SERIOUSLY... YOU HAVE TO LAUGH

Great yarns and tall tales from the sporting fields, dressing rooms and commentary boxes of Australia

PETER FITZSIMONS

ALLEN&UNWIN

SYDNEY • MELBOURNE • AUCKLAND • LONDON

First published in 2016

Allen & Unwin
83 Alexander Street
Crows Nest NSW 2065
Australia
Phone: (61 2) 8425 0100
Email: info@allenandunwin.com
Web: www.allenandunwin.com

Cataloguing-in-Publication details are available from the National Library of
Australia
www.trove.nla.gov.au

ISBN 978 1 76029 399 4

Set in 12/17 pt Minion Pro by Midland Typesetters, Australia
Printed and bound in Australia by Griffin Press

10 9 8 7 6 5 4 3 2 1

Other works by Peter FitzSimons

Basking in Beirut and Other Adventures with Peter FitzSimons
Nick Farr Jones
Rugby Stories
Hitch-hiking for Ugly People
The Rugby War
Everyone but Phar Lap
Everyone and Phar Lap
FitzSimons on Rugby
Beazley
Nancy Wake
John Eales
Nene
Kokoda
The Story of Skilled and Frank Hargrave
Steve Waugh
Great Australian Sports Champions
Little Theories of Life
The Ballad of Les Darcy
Tobruk
Kokoda
And Now for Some Light Relief
Charles Kingsford Smith and Those Magnificent Men
A Simpler Time
Mawson
Batavia
Eureka
Ned Kelly
Carlo Salteri and the Story of Transfield
Gallipoli
Fromelles and Pozières

INTRODUCTION

On the 30 May 2016, I marked up 30 years since I began writing for the mighty *Sydney Morning Herald*. I love the paper, its people and its readers in equal measure—and have never lost the sense of privilege I had on that first day to be published in such a mighty journal. Over that time, I guess about 75 per cent of my output has been in the sports pages and, within that realm, I have been frequently attracted to the funny yarns, the hilarious dressing-room stories, the killer quotes that you just don't see coming. I have found that readers love that kind of stuff far more than accounts of who won what and why, and as I love writing that stuff more than the other it is a happy coincidence.

I am indebted to many of those readers who have sent me such yarns over the years. It takes us all back to what sport was meant to be in the first place—fun.

I do hope you enjoy this collection of the funniest stuff I have written, and gathered, over the years.

Peter FitzSimons
August 2016
Neutral Bay

Addressing the balls

The following notice was prominently displayed at a popular suburban golf club.

1. Back straight, knees bent, feet shoulder-width apart.

2. Form a loose grip.

3. Keep your head down!

4. Avoid a quick backswing.

5. Stay out of the water.

6. Try not to hit anyone.

7. If you are taking too long, let others go ahead of you.

8. Don't stand directly in front of others.

9. Quiet, please ... while others are preparing.

10. Don't take extra strokes.

Well done ... Now, flush the urinal, wash your hands, go outside and tee off.

Taking pains

And then, of course, there is the story of the famed hard man of rugby league in the 1960s, Kevin Ryan. One time, while playing a home game for St George at Kogarah Oval against the Manly Sea Eagles, Ryan executed such a devastating tackle against the Manly prop that he dislocated his shoulder and knocked the prop into the middle of next week.

Both men were rushed straight to St George Hospital, where a young doctor tried to put Ryan's shoulder back in. Now, although not usually a man to even grimace when in pain, this action by the young doctor was so agonising that the surprised Ryan did indeed let out a loud cry.

Seeing an opportunity to take down a peg or two this esteemed representative of the very footballing breed she had never warmed to, Matron scolded him: 'Why, Mr Ryan, that is not necessary. I have just come from delivering Mrs Smither's baby in the next ward, and she didn't make half as much noise!'

'Really?' growled Ryan in reply. 'Let's see what kind of noise she'd make if they tried to put the baby back in!'

Thai this on

At the Rugby World Cup of 2011, an Englishman, a Scotsman, an Irishman, a Welshman, a Gurkha, a Latvian, a Turk, an Aussie, a German, a Yank, an Egyptian, a Japanese, a Mexican, a Spaniard, a Russian, a Pole, a Lithuanian, a Jordanian, a Kiwi, a Swede, a Finn, an Israeli, a Romanian, a Bulgarian, a Serb, a Swiss, a Greek, a Singaporean, an Italian, a Norwegian, an Argentinian, a Libyan, a Pakistani, an Indian, a Chinese, a Macedonian, a Ukrainian and an African all turn up together at a swish Wellington nightclub.

'Sorry,' the bouncer says, glaring at them balefully, 'I can't let you in without a Thai.'

Bait and switch

The last time the Pope was in Australia he found himself beside a river in the Northern Territory when a sudden commotion on the far shore attracted his attention. Holy Mary! Right there, in the jaws of a massive crocodile, is a man wearing an All Black jersey desperately struggling to get free. Suddenly three blokes wearing Wallaby jerseys roar into view on a speedboat. The first bloke fires a harpoon into the croc's ribs, while the other two reach over and pull the Kiwi from the river before, using long clubs, they beat the croc to death. They are bundling the bleeding, semi-conscious man into the speedboat when ... What the ...?

They notice someone.

Bugger me. It is bloke on the bank wearing a small white beanie. He calls out to them in this thick accent: 'I had heard that there was a racist xenophobic divide between Australia and New Zealand, but now I have seen with my own eyes that this is not true. I can see that your societies are true examples of racial harmony and could serve as a model that other nations could follow.' With which, he blessed them and drove off in a cloud of dust.

As he departs the harpoonist turns to the other Aussies and asks: 'Who the bloody hell was that?'

'That,' one answered, 'was his Holiness the Pope. He is in direct contact with God.'

'Well,' the harpoonist sagely replies, 'he knows f**k-all about croc hunting! Now, will this bait still do, or do we need to get another one?'

King of the quickie

Wayne Carey and Mark Bickley are enjoying a lunch at a fancy West Lakes restaurant. The waitress approaches their table to take their order. She is young and very attractive. She asks Bickley what he wants and he replies, 'I'll have the heart-healthy salad.'

'Very good, sir,' she says. Turning to Carey she asks: 'And what do you want, Wayne?'

Carey answers: 'How 'bout a quickie?'

Taken aback, the waitress slaps him and says: 'I'm shocked and disappointed in you. I thought you were on the straight and narrow and committed to high principles and morality, not like last year.' With that, the waitress departs in a huff.

In the stunned silence that follows, Bickley leans over to Carey and says: 'Actually, Wayne, I believe that's pronounced "quiche".'

———

I feel obliged to pass on to you the results of a recent poll in Melbourne which asked 1000 women if they would ever sleep with Wayne Carey.

72 per cent replied: 'Never again!'

———

Shortly after the Wayne Carey blow-up in 2002, a North Melbourne supporter wrote to *The Age*, in misery: 'This has been the worst year of my life. First 9/11 and now this.'

Best's dry run

The great George Best was once asked why he left Manchester United in the early '70s to go to play in the ill-fated American Soccer League.

'Because,' Best replied, 'I was walking along Kings Road in Chelsea one day and a London bus went past with the advertisement "DRINK CANADA DRY" ... so I did.'

———

After Best's fall from grace in the '70s he played briefly for various no-name clubs in England and Scotland, and was given a final 'last chance' in America with the Tampa Bay Rowdies or some such. At the time he was still escorting a former Miss World.

On a rare weekend off, the couple went to Las Vegas, where George had a big win at the tables—a small recompense for all the money he'd previously lost, but anyway. Back in his room he ordered a nightcap of French champagne and some caviar.

The room-service waiter, a fellow native of Belfast, arrived to see George was sitting on the bed counting a huge pile of $100 and $1,000 notes as his partner emerged from the bathroom in a slinky negligee.

The waiter looked at the money, the girl, the champagne and caviar and said: 'Tell me this, George, just where *exactly* did it all start to go wrong for you?'

Woods Wonder

Stevie Wonder and Tiger Woods are in a bar. Stevie asks Tiger how his golf is going.

Tiger replies, 'I've had some problems with my swing, but I think it's okay now.'

Stevie says, 'I always find that when my swing goes wrong, I need to stop playing for a while and not think about it.'

Tiger says, 'You play *golf*?'

Stevie says, 'Yes, I've been playing for years.'

Tiger says, 'But—you're blind! How can you play golf if you can't see?'

Stevie Wonder replies, 'Well, I get my caddy to stand in the middle of the fairway and call to me. I listen for the sound of his voice and play the ball towards him.'

'But, how do you putt?' asks Tiger.

'Well,' says Stevie, 'I get my caddy to lean down in front of the hole and call to me with his head on the ground and I just play the ball towards his voice.'

Tiger asks, 'What's your handicap?'

Stevie says, 'Well, actually, I'm a scratch golfer.'

Tiger, incredulous, says to Stevie, 'We've got to play a round some time.'

Wonder replies, 'Well, people don't take me seriously, so I only play for money and never play for less than ten thousand dollars a hole. That a problem?'

Woods thinks about it and says, 'Okay, I'm game for that. Ten thousand a hole is fine with me. When would you like to play?'

Stevie says, 'Pick a night.'

Seven easy steps

With the ski season upon us, I have been sent the following bits of training advice for those getting ready to hit the slopes.

1. Visit local butcher and pay $30 to sit in the walk-in freezer for 30 minutes. Afterwards, burn two $50 dollar bills to warm up.

2. Throw away a $100 bill—now.

3. Find the nearest ice rink and walk across the ice 20 times in your ski boots carrying two pairs of skis, accessory bag and poles. Pretend you are looking for your car. Sporadically drop things.

4. Place a small but angular pebble in your shoes, line them with crushed ice, and then tighten a C-clamp around your toes.

5. Go to McDonald's and insist on paying $8.50 for a hamburger. Be sure you are in the longest line.

6. Dress up in as many clothes as you can and then proceed to take them off because you have to go to the bathroom.

7. Slam your thumb in a car door. Don't go see a doctor.

That hurts

The following exchange took place on ABC Radio during the second of the one-day internationals between Australia and the West Indies, after the Australian vice-captain took a fearful ball to the groin.

Commentator 1 (concerned): 'Michael Clarke's in a lot of pain. The West Indies' wicketkeeper is offering some sympathy.'

Commentator 2: 'Ricky Ponting is wandering down to see how his vice-captain is.'

Commentator 1 (indignant tone): 'Ricky's just tapped Clarkey on the bum with his bat ...'

Commentator 2: 'Probably knocking them back out ...'

Masochism training

After last week's rant on things one could do to prepare for the skiing season—join the longest queue at McDonald's and finally get to pay an exorbitant price for a hamburger—a reader suggests how to prepare to play rugby union:

1. Find large pool of mud. Dive into it.

2. Find large friend. Have him beat you up.

3. Walk to first floor window. Jump out.

4. Buy a whistle. Have a friend blow it at you constantly for 80 minutes.

5. Have a friend practise goal kicking, while you stand around watching until your nose bleeds.

Remembering Richie

A few favourite Benaud moments:

Bruce Reid was coming out to bat, with Australia still a few runs short of victory in a one-day match.

Richie, dry as the Nullarbor: 'Well, Bruce Reid is not the worst batsman there is at international level ... but those who are worse would not need to hire the Myer Music Bowl to hold a convention.'

———

Richie Benaud, as dry as his favourite martini, when NSW batsman Corey Richards was being treated for an injury high on his leg, in a match against South Australia: 'It's either a groin or a hamstring. Don't know which is worse ... it's been so long since I've pulled either.'

———

Co-commentator: 'He has been struggling with tennis elbow.'

Richie (in his driest tone): 'Now, what's a nice boy like that doing with tennis elbow?'

That's a handy contribution

Jim Muir recently took his nine-year-old daughter Lucy to see an A-League match. The referee had made some unpopular decisions and, of course, the chant went up from the crowd that: 'The referee's a wanker, the referee's a wanker ...'

It was at this point that Lucy turned to her father and asked the obvious question: 'What's a wanker, Dad?'

Her question, put loudly in the voice of one whose very innocence penetrated the atmosphere all around, reduced the fans close by to a stunned silence. How was Dad going to answer this? They leaned forward, as each second struck like thunder and our man Jim went through a variety of possible answers before rejecting each one.

And then an angel appeared, in the form of a large Scotsman, positioned just two seats away. 'A wanker,' he said, 'is a man who prefers his own company!'

Rough end

A bodybuilder appeared on Bert Newton's *Family Feud* and was asked to name a vegetable starting with 'P'. His answer was 'Pineapple.'

But, better still, apparently in the early '90s, in an earlier incarnation of *Family Feud*, a fellow called Graham was asked to 'Name a food that makes a noise when you eat it'.

'Baked beans,' he replied confidently.

Young & desperate

Back in 2001, Judith Lucy and I were among a group who appeared in a series of Channel Nine 'Super Debates.' One of the topics was 'That the Aussie Bloke is a Hopeless Joke,' and in the course of her electrifying speech she recounted how, many years ago, she was dinkum doing a Saturday-night gig with the famed lesbian comedian Sue-Ann Post, oddly enough at a local Aussie Rules club in western Victoria.

It is getting late by the time Sue-Ann Post comes on stage, and her solid-male audience is nothing if not well-oiled. 'Show us yer tits!' they roar.

A professional, with great experience dealing with unruly crowds, Post ploughs on into her routine regardless and is soon getting good laughs. And yet some of the crowd would not be quelled.

'Show us yer tits!' they insist.

Again, Post ploughs on and again soon has more of the crowd with her than before. Still, however, the most drunken of the lot will not be denied.

'SHOW US YER TITS!'

This time, Post can stand it no more and roars back at the hecklers, 'Oh, for God's sake, I'm a *lesbian!*'

Stunned silence, only broken when a few seconds later a seventeen-year-old boy from up the back forlornly calls out, 'Oh, go on, show us anyway?'

Quick-witted

Former Celtic coach Gordon Strachan was once buttonholed in the tunnel by a reporter after a devastating loss.

Reporter: 'Gordon, can I have a quick word?'

Strachan (without breaking stride): 'Velocity.'

On yer way

916

Former New Zealand Test wicketkeeper Ian Smith recalls an incident that occurred during a Test between England and New Zealand.

Way back when Smith is batting against England, a fast ball gets through and hits him in the netheries. He falls down, sees stars and then hears pained titters from all the fielders around, glad that it wasn't them.

Then he looks up and sees the concerned face of legendary umpire Dickie Bird above him.

'Are thee OK, lad?' Dicky asks kindly.

'I think so,' Smith groans.

'Can thee get up and walk, lad?' the sympathetic umpire asks.

'I think so,' said Smith, still in exquisite agony.

'Then walk lad,' Bird said. 'You're out LBW.'

Fickle finger of fate

And now for the most classic example of our time of the terrible damage that can be done by a simple misunderstanding. It is of course the distasteful John Hopoate episode, where he rose to notoriety around the world for using his fingers in the tackle.

It was a story that led the CNN sports news, received a full page in the London *Daily Mail* and was even picked up by the *South China Morning Post*, not to mention wall-to-wall coverage around the clock, and around the country, for weeks on end in Australia.

And yet it all could have been so different.

If only Hopoate had properly understood what his coach had meant that day just before they played the Gold Coast Titans, when the coach had put his arm around him and said, 'Today, Hoppa, I want you to make your mark in the annals of rugby league.'

———

Ray Churchill, Tokyo: 'I'm so old that I can remember when the words "sports update" had absolutely no connection with John Hopoate.'

23

Smart Bart

When Darren Beadman informed Bart Cummings that he had 'spoken to God' and God had told him he wanted him to quit being a jockey to join the ministry, the great trainer considered this for a few moments and then advised the small man in front of him: 'I think you should seek a second opinion.'

Cummings, deadpan, yonks ago to a health inspector, who narkily told him he had too many flies in his stables: 'How many flies am I allowed to have?'

———

A couple of years ago, Bart comes in for a haircut just before the Spring Carnival. Has to be looking his best for the usual slew of trophies to put upon his groaning mantelpiece, likely the most over-worked bit of woodwork in the country.

Anyhoo, the barber does the usual splendid job, being very careful not to touch a single hair on those splendid eyebrows, and finally finishes, before—of course—asking Bart for a tip for the coming racing carnival.

Carefully, Bart opens his wallet, takes out a crisp lobster, a lovely new $20 note, looks him right in the eye, and says 'NEVER GAMBLE.'

The jaws of victory

Four days into the Sydney Olympics the wrestling event gets underway at Darling Harbour. In the heavyweight division, after three days of eliminations, it comes down to the famous Russian wrestler Igor Medvedev and the American Hank Ruth for the gold medal.

Before the final match, the American wrestler's coach comes to him and says, 'Now, Hank, don't forget all the research we've done on this Russian. In twenty years, he's never lost a match because of that "pretzel" hold he has. Whatever you do, don't let him get you in that hold. If he does, you're finished!'

Hank, a good ol' boy from Arkansas, nods tightly. He understands.

And then, at 3 pm on the afternoon of 22 September 2000, they get to it. The American and the Russian circle each other several times, looking for an opening. And there it is! Though Medvedev is a big bear of a man, he moves as quickly as a panther and in an instant he has sprung on the American, taken him down to the mat and wrapped him up in the dreaded pretzel hold!

From the stands, it is clear that Hank Ruth is so impossibly contorted—with arms and legs everywhere, and all of them at impossible angles to his torso—in the Russian's deadly grip that the result is now inevitable. It can only be a matter of seconds before Hank's shoulders are pinned, and a deep sigh of disappointment goes up. Hank's coach buries his face in his hands, unable to watch the totally predictable ending.

Suddenly, though, Medvedev lets out a blood-curdling scream and Hank Ruth is seen to bounce high from the mat like a tightly coiled spring that has been unleashed! A resounding cheer goes up from the crowd and the trainer raises his eyes just in time to see first the Russian flop weakly back onto the mat and then Hank weakly collapse on top of him, securing the pin in a few seconds and winning the match and the Olympic gold medal.

The trainer is astounded! When he finally gets Hank alone, he asks, 'How did you ever get out of that hold? No one has ever done it before!'

Hank, still pale from exhaustion and shaking, rasps out, 'Well, I was ready to give up when he got me in that hold, but at the last moment I opened my eyes and saw this pair of balls right in front of my face. I thought I had nothing to lose, so with my last ounce of strength I stretched out my neck and bit those babies just as hard as I could …

'Coach, you'd be amazed how strong you get when you bite your own balls!'

Mistaken, moi?

When Marty Roebuck was on tour with the Wallabies in France in 1989, he notices a fly in his soup in a Toulon restaurant.

Deciding this was a good moment to practise his St Stanislaus schoolboy French, he summons a waiter and says, pointing to the little beastie: '*Le mouche!*'

The waiter could not help himself and corrects Marty, saying: '*Monsieur, c'est la mouche.*'

'What?' says Marty.

'*C'est la mouche, parce que c'est feminine …*'

Marty looks closer … 'Good God, man, you've good eyesight!'

———

Somewhat similarly, at a Russian restaurant in Sydney some years ago a reader's friend tried to impress with his knowledge of Russian and ordered in Russian.

The waiter replied, 'And how would you like your 1000 yellow pencil boxes cooked, sir?'

Wisdom of the racetrack

Peter Moody, trainer of Black Caviar: 'You know what I'd love to do? I'd like to win the lotto, buy a 5 per cent share in a racehorse and drive the trainer mad by ringing up every night to see how it's going. I'd be doing that while lying on a beach in far north Queensland eating prawns and drinking beer. I'd have my fourth wife—a 21-year-old six-foot blonde—stroking my overgrown stomach and I'd stay up there until I died from a massive heart attack with a cigarette in my mouth.'

—

Herald letter-writer David Atherfold: 'As my late father often told me, "Son, the only one to make money out of following the horses is the bloke with the shovel".'

Sherves him right

The story goes that Sean Connery had fallen on hard times but brightened immeasurably when he got a call from his agent.

The agent said: 'Sean, I've got a job for you. Starts tomorrow, but you've got to get there early, for 10-ish.'

Sean frowned, and replied: 'Ten-ish? But I haven't even got a racquet…'

Many a slip

As rugby tragics will not need to be reminded, the 2007 Rugby World Cup was held in France. And, against all expectations, BOTH the All Blacks and the Wallabies were knocked out in the quarter-finals. But at least the losers had a few jokes to share between gritted teeth:

Latest news from the Rugby World Cup 2007 ...
England to meet France in the first semi-final.
South Africa to meet Argentina in the other semi-final.
Australia to meet New Zealand at the airport.

———

Q. If the World Cup finalists play for the William Webb Ellis Trophy, what is the name of the trophy played for by the teams finishing seventh and eighth?
A. The Bledisloe Cup!

———

Q. What did the All Blacks do as their contribution to limiting the emissions that cause global warming?
A. Dropped the Wallabies off on the way home!

———

Q. What's the difference between the All Blacks and a tea-bag?
A. The tea-bag stays in the cup longer.

—

Q. How do you get a champagne cork back into the bottle?
A. Ask any Aussie supporter ...

Mixed massages

Two women are playing golf on a sunny afternoon when one of them slices her shot into a foursome of men. To her horror, one of the men collapses in agony with both hands in his crotch. She runs to him apologising profusely, explaining that she is a physical therapist and can help ease his pain.

'No, thanks … just give me a few minutes … I'll be fine …' he replies quietly with his hands still between his legs.

Taking it upon herself to help the poor man, she gently undoes the front of his pants and starts massaging his genitals. 'Doesn't that feel better?' she asks.

'Well … yes … that feels pretty good,' he admits. 'But my thumb still hurts like hell.'

An inspirational story

Recently, I was asked to play in a golf tournament.

At first, I said, 'Naaahhh!'

Then they said to me, 'Come on, it's for handicapped and blind kids.'

Then I thought, 'F**k, I could win this!'

———

Bob Hope to a friendly golf pro: 'What is the easiest way to knock seven strokes off my total?'

The pro's deadpan reply: 'Miss one of the par threes.'

———

Back in the day, we would always say of Wallaby captain Simon Poidevin that his golf game was the exact model of his rugby game: 'Always the first to the ball.'

Gatekeeper & Coe

It is just a couple of minutes before the opening ceremony of the Sydney 2000 Olympic Games, and one of the most distinguished British athletes of all time, Sebastian Coe, arrives at the gates in a whole flurry of hurry. He has been caught in dreadful traffic and is determined not to miss a second of the ceremony.

Alas, he has turned up at gate A, when his pass allows him access only through gate N, which is right on the other side of the stadium. The gatekeeper refuses to allow him access.

'Look,' says Lord Coe, 'do you have any idea who I am? I am Lord Sebastian Coe, world-record holder in the eight hundred metres and fifteen hundred metres and three-time Olympic gold medallist!'

The steward looks him up and down and says nonchalantly, 'Shouldn't take you long to get to gate N then, should it?'

Roids

The ambitious coach of a girls track team gives the squad steroids. The team's performance soars. They win the county and state championship, and then one day they are favoured to win the nationals easily.

Penelope, a sixteen-year-old hurdler, visits her coach and says, straight out, 'Coach, I have a problem. Hair is starting to grow on my chest.'

'*What?*' the coach says in a panic. 'How far down does it go?'

'Down to my balls,' she replies, 'and that's something else I want to talk to you about.'

My b-b-b-brother Don

Former Queensland bowler Bill Tallon was the brother of Don Tallon, who was both the Australian and Queensland wicket-keeper. Bill had a terrible stutter, but that never prevented him telling all and sundry, on any occasion, about his favourite game with 'my b-b-b-brother Don'.

In that time before the Second World War, Queensland were playing South Australia in a crucial Sheffield game at the Gabba, and Bill was tossed the ball to send down the opening thunderbolts.

'The man on strike was a left-hander by the n-n-n-name of Nitschke,' Bill relates, 'and I b-b-b-bowled this b-b-b-beautiful in-swinger to him and it just n-n-n-nicked his bat. My b-b-b-brother Don dived to his left and t-t-t-took in front of first slip. B-b-b-bloody beauty! South Australia were 1/0!'

The next batsman in was Clayvel Badcock and the Queens-landers were not long in getting stuck into him. Bill kept peppering him with bouncers and yorkers and Badcock started getting frustrated.

'And then I b-b-b-bowled a b-b-b-beautiful out-swinger at him. He snicked it, and my b-b-b-brother Don dived a long way to his right and t-t-t-took it in front of second slip. B-b-b-bloody beauty! 2/0!'

The next one in for South Australia was this cove, Bradman. True, he was a different kettle of fish altogether, but finally Bill had worked him out.

'I b-b-b-bowled a b-b-b-bouncer and that fellow B-B-B-Bradman went for a hook. The ball went so high that fine-leg ran for it, mid-on ran for it, square-leg ran for it and I ran for it. It was still so high that I got sunburned on the b-b-b-back of my throat waiting for it to come down. But, b-b-b-bloody beauty, my b-b-b-brother Don took over and made sure of the catch. *B-B-B-BLOODY BEAUTY! Got him! 3/411!*'

Who were the only father and son to play Test cricket simultaneously?

(Careful it might be a trick.) Answer below.

Quiz answer: Miandad.

Sledger slayed

In 1999, the Australian team are playing Zimbabwe, when one of the Australian bowlers keeps narrowly missing getting the portly Zimbabwean tail-ender Eddo Brandes out. Finally, it is more than flesh and blood can stand, and when Brandes misses the ball completely one more time, still without giving up his wicket, the Australian bowler finishes just a couple of metres from the Zimbabwean batsman.

'Why are you so fat?' the bowler snarls, glaring at Brandes.

The reply comes back in an instant: 'Because every time I f**k your wife, she gives me a biscuit.'

It's three minutes before the Australian slips cordon can again compose themselves well enough for the bowler to deliver his next ball.

The greatest sledge of all time

So now it's official. After 19 seasons, the great NBA player Karl Malone—known as The Mailman, because he always delivered—is retiring at age 41. Over that time he has swished 36,928 points (second only to Kareem Abdul-Jabbar's 38,387). Is that what he'll be remembered for, though? At least in part. But he will also go down as the man on the receiving end of one of the great American sporting sledges of all time.

It's a Sunday evening and game one of the 1997 NBA finals, see. The Chicago Bulls are in scoring lock-step with Malone's Utah Jazz and the crowd is roaring. The last grains of sand are trickling through the hourglass and the nation has stopped, watching. Then FOUL!

Karl Malone, the great one, gets to go to the free-throw line for two shots—practically a gift of two points for a player of his calibre. The Jazz are home!

Now, though, as the Bulls and Jazz players take their places around the key, the Bulls' Scottie Pippen sidles past and says mildly to Malone: 'The Mailman don't deliver on Sundays ...'

Malone misses both shots and the Bulls win.

A moving story

Collingwood coach Mick Malthouse gets wind of a potential young recruit who lives, of all places, in Iraq. Malthouse and the recruiting manager catch a plane and, risking life and limb, track him down. Turns out the kid is a genius. Can thread a ball through the posts from sixty metres! They take him back to Collingwood, and he is picked on the bench for the first match of this year.

Ten minutes into the first quarter, forward Chris Tarrant goes down with a severe knee injury. Malthouse turns to the boy and says: 'This is it, son. Go to centre half-forward and show us what you can do.'

The boy proceeds to make an extraordinary debut for one who only a year previously had never even seen an AFL game. He kicks five goals, takes the best mark of the year, and nails the winning goal from 45 metres out, after the siren.

In the dressing room the delighted Malthouse hands the kid his mobile phone and tells him to ring his mother to tell her just how great he has been.

'Mum,' the kid says. 'Guess what I did today?'

But before he can go on, his mother sobs: 'Let me tell you about our day. Your father has been stabbed and robbed, our house has been torched, our car blown up and your brother abducted.'

'Gee,' says the boy, 'I'm really sorry.'

'You should be,' his mother replies. 'If it wasn't for you, we would never have shifted to Collingwood.'

In Tiger Woods' heyday

You might remember that quote from an American comedian in early 2003, at a time when Tiger Woods was at his most rampant—on the golf course too.

'You know the world's gone crazy when the best golfer is a black guy, the best rapper is a white guy, Switzerland has the America's Cup ... and Germany doesn't want to fight this war.'

———

On a golf tour in Ireland, Tiger Woods drives his Mercedes-Benz into a petrol station, just on the edge of a picturesque rural village.

The attendant at the pump greets him in a typical Irish manner, completely unaware of who the golfing pro is.

'Top of the morning to ya,' says the attendant.

Tiger nods a quick, cursory 'hello' and bends forward to pick up the nozzle. As he does so, two tees fall out of his shirt pocket.

'What are dey den, son?' asks the attendant.

'They're called tees,' replies Tiger.

'Well, what are dey for?' inquires the Irishman.

'They're for resting my balls on when I'm driving,' says Tiger.

'Frickin' Jaysus,' says this son of the Emerald Isle. 'Dem boys at Mercedes tink of everything.'

———

Q. What is a hundred white men chasing one black man the definition of?
A. The USPGA Golf Tour.

———

Stuart Appleby, during a Masters, being asked what he felt he needed to shoot on the fourth day to be considered a chance of winning: 'Tiger Woods.'

He didn't, and Tiger won it.

Kiwi fans went ape in
brass monkey weather.

Kiwi fans went ape in brass monkey weather

You have to imagine the scene in Christchurch last weekend. It was so cold the only creatures out were polar bears, mad dogs, Wallabies, All Blacks and rugby fans.

At half-time the Wallabies were losing 6-3, and in the men's toilets, hordes of frozen but exuberant men dressed in black stood shivering, waiting their turn.

Now, a couple of Wallaby fans in their gold jerseys come in and some thick-necked Kiwi yells out: 'How're you feeling now, you Aussies?'

Without a beat the confident (and rather large) Aussie says: 'We can't lose, mate. We get to go home tomorrow.'

Cricket ball

This bloke goes to the doctor. 'Doc, I've got a cricket ball stuck up my bottom.'

'How's that?'

'Don't you start!'

Packer dobber

Back in the mid-1980s one April, the redoubtable Darrell Eastlake is working away on a Saturday morning in the *Wide World of Sports* cottage in Scott Street, Willoughby, when the phone rings.

He picks it up, only to hear that famous growl: 'How's Easter going?'

It is Kerry Packer, calling all the way from London!

'Terrific, Mr Packer, terrific,' Big Dazza replies quickly, trying to gather himself, 'the sun's shining, the surf's up, had a great barbie with the kids yesterday, played a bit of frisbee ...'

Eastlake got only as far as this when he is interrupted by a mighty roar: 'Not that f***ing Easter you f***ing IDIOT! My Easter, my horse Easter, running in the Randwick carnival! Who am I f***ing TALKING to!?!?'

Darrell takes a deep breath, looks left, looks right. It simply has to be done. He doesn't want to do it, but it HAS to be done.

'Ken Sutcliffe, Mr Packer, goodbye.'

(Click.)

What's in a name?

The following was posted by a fan on a Sheffield United website:

'I'm feeling all angry about these modern-day footballers. I know why they've gone all soft. It's because of poncy names. That's what it is.

'Remember in the old days, when footy players kicked a f***ing ball made out of ten pound of clay stitched inside a steel-reinforced leather shell with laces made out of piano wire? Well, in them days players could only survive the rigours of the game because they were called things like Arthur, Bert, Harry, Bill, Bob, Jack and Tommy.

'And what do we have now? Jason, Wayne, Dean, Ryan, Jamie, Robbie. F***ing tarts' names, they are. No wonder the ball's like a f***ing balloon and shin pads is like slices of bread.

'In the old days you never saw a Len Shackleton or a Billy Wright with a puffy little Sondico piece of paper down his little thin socks. F***ing shinpads in them days was made out of library books, and socks was like sackcloth.

'Same with the jerseys—f***ing shirts with holes in now, so they can breathe. Yes, so that little Jody's hairless chest can breathe and he doesn't get a chill. Stanley Matthews used to dribble round Europe's finest wearing a f***ing tent and shorts cobbled together from the jacket of his de-mob suit.

'So I say we start calling kids real male names again. Otherwise what we gonna get in twenty years' time? The England team full of players called Keanu, Ronan, Ashley and f***ing Chesney.'

I think he sounds sincere.

Holey Moses

A rabbi is out of town on Yom Kippur. Since nobody knows who he is, he decides to play a round of golf. Up in heaven, God, who has been busy on the day sorting out Jarryd Haynes' next move, doesn't catch up with what has happened until the rabbi sinks his putt on the 15th.

He decides to punish him for playing golf on the holiest of all holy days, but is stopped by Moses, who says: 'Let me take care of this.'

God thinks about it for a moment and says 'OK.'

So the rabbi tees off on the 16th and, from above, Moses causes the ball to be such a flawless shot it lands a perfect hole in one.

This is repeated on the 17th and 18th, the only time in the history of the world there have been three successive aces.

God, staggered, turns to Moses and says: 'I thought you were going to punish him!?!?'

Moses replies: 'Who's he going to tell?'

Wisdom at the game played in heaven

'Losing to NSW is like losing a golf ball or masturbating. You hate yourself when you've done it, but you know you'll do it again.' Queensland's own Chris 'Buddha' Handy

'A warm-up to me was a cigarette just before you went on. I reckoned if you did five sprints when you went on to the paddock that was five sprints you wouldn't do during the game.' Stan Pilecki, former Wallabies prop, reminiscing about the grand old days

'It's like they say, "Play rugby union and see the world. Play rugby league and see Wigan …"' Wallabies World Cup-winning prop Richard Harry

'Plenty of the blokes from the NSW Country side played for Australia and we've kept in touch. Unlike the blokes from the '60s, who all married each other's wives, we're all pretty close.' Greg Cornelsen

Nick Cummins, the Honey Badger, on how to beat the Waratahs: 'You've got to be like a midget in the urinals, you've got to be on your toes.'

A boy, a dog and a blasted reporter

Two little boys are playing kick-to-kick in a park in Sydney's Eastern Suburbs when one of them is attacked by a vicious Rottweiler. Thinking quickly, the other boy grabs a branch, wedges it down the dog's collar and twists, luckily breaking the dog's neck and stopping its attack.

A reporter who was strolling by sees the incident and rushes over to interview the boy. 'Young Rooster Fan Saves Friend From Vicious Animal,' he starts writing in his notebook.

'But I'm not a Rooster fan,' the little hero replies.

'Sorry, since we are in the Eastern Suburbs, I just assumed you were,' says the reporter and starts again. 'Young Rabbits Fan Rescues Friend from Horrific Attack,' he continues writing in his notebook.

'I'm not a Rabbits fan either!' the boy says.

'I assumed everyone in the Eastern Suburbs was either for the Roosters or the Rabbits,' the reporter replies. 'So what team DO you barrack for?'

'I'm a Bulldogs fan!' the child beams proudly.

The reporter starts a new sheet in his notebook and writes, 'Little Bugger from Canterbury Kills Beloved Family Pet.'

Barred for life

This is one of my favourite lines of the year. It concerns a bloke by the name of Richard Bortkevich, 26, who is the son of famous Olympic gymnast Olga Korbut. Last week, alas, in Lawrenceville, Georgia, police raided Bortkevich's apartment and found $US20,000 ($36,200) in fake $US100 bills, and he has since pleaded guilty to counterfeiting.

You tell 'em, Dwight Perry, of the *Seattle Times*: 'Possible punishments include, fittingly enough, a lot of parallel bars.'

That's a tall call

There's this American, see, and he decides to write a book about famous churches around the world, starting with Australia and New Zealand. One plane trip later and he's in a Sydney church snapping shots when he notices a golden telephone mounted on the wall beneath a sign that reads '$10,000 per call'.

The American, intrigued, asks the priest and is informed it's a direct line to heaven and that for $10,000 you could talk to God hisself in heaven! Amazed, the American nevertheless finds the same thing in Brisbane, Perth, Melbourne, Adelaide, Hobart and Darwin. Each time, a golden telephone beneath a sign saying '$10,000 per call', and a curate who swears on the head of Mother Mary that for that price heaven was on the line.

But now there's a funny thing. As soon as he'd landed in Wellington, and gone to their best cathedral, there was the same golden telephone beneath a similar sign, but this time the price demanded was only 10¢. The American was surprised, so he asked the priest about the sign:

'Father, I've travelled all over Australia and I've seen this same golden telephone in many churches. I'm told that it is a direct line to heaven, but in all the cities in Australia the price was $10,000 per call. Why is it so cheap here?'

The priest smiled and answered: 'You're in New Zealand now, son, it's a local call.'

Carn Panfers!

I bow to no one in my admiration for Penrith: the town, the team and its people. And that is precisely why I reprint below a couple of bits from an email that has been doing the rounds. I do so to show just what elitist mongrel dogs some people are, and also in the knowledge (read hope) that Penrith people are not so uptight they can't laugh along at the printable parts of 'You Know You're a Panfers Supporter When ...'

1. You think Dom Perignon is a Mafia leader.

2. A ceiling fan once ruined your wife's hairdo.

3. You think the last words of Advance Australia Fair are: 'Carn Panfers.'

4. The market value of your car goes up and down, depending on how much petrol is in it.

5. Your toilet paper has page numbers on it.

Tombstone territory

Two blokes are walking through a cemetery when they happen upon a tombstone that reads: 'Here lies John Sweeney, a good man and a rugby fan.'

So one of them asks the other: 'When the hell did they start putting more than one person in a grave?'

Mum's the word

At a recent junior soccer game things are really starting to get out of hand. It gets so bad that at one point the coach calls one of his seven-year-old players aside and asks: 'Do you understand what "co-operation" is? What a "team" is?'

The little boy nods.

'Do you understand that what matters is whether we win or lose together as a team?'

The little boy nods.

'So,' the coach continues, 'I'm sure you know, when a foul is called, you shouldn't argue, curse, attack the referee, or call him a "dickhead". Do you understand all that?'

Again the little boy nods.

He continues: 'And when I take you out of the game so another boy gets a chance to play, it's not good sportsmanship to call your coach "a dumb arsehole", is it?'

Again the little boy nods.

'Good,' says the coach. 'Now go over there and explain all that to your mother.'

Cometti classic

Some years ago, I was honoured to be asked by the great man, Dennis Cometti, to write the foreword for a book of his best one-liners, as I have long loved his pearls and proclaimed to the world exactly that. Here's a brief selection of some of the best:

When the Hawks' wayward kicking cost them a game against Geelong they should have won: 'They'll be kicking themselves right now. But with their luck, they'd probably miss.'

'The Dockers defence is in disarray. Everybody wants to be Gladys Knight; nobody wants to be the Pips.'

'When the Saints kicked that goal, I was watching those Bulldog defenders and they just fanned out like a group of crazed Amway salesmen.'

'There's Koutoufides. More vowels than possessions today.'

'Look at Long. That's a sweat! Like Marlon Brando eating Thai food!'

'Scotty Cummings alone in the square, jumping up and down and waving his arms like they're playing "My Sharona".'

'The goal square's full of Bears. Looks like we've got ourselves a convoy.'

'If it was a set play, they copied it from a Portuguese bus timetable.'

Gerard Healy, commentating during a Melbourne v. Collingwood match: 'Word is this guy is the most reliable kick for goal in the side. They say down at Collingwood if you had to have someone kicking for your life, Tarkyn Lockyer would be the man ...'

Cometti: 'I'd prefer my mum.' (Silence) 'Not a great footballer, but at least she'd care.'

During a Geelong v. Essendon match the Bombers succeeded in belting the ball forward and Andrew Lovett ran into an open goal, booting the ball hard and low into the Geelong cheer squad. He then tried to appease the angry mob. 'Well, Lovett was apologising,' Cometti said. 'He didn't intend for the shot to hit the fan!'

Cometti's on-air account of his first meeting with Channel Nine's Eddie McGuire, when Eddie was the CEO of Channel Nine: 'Ed had an aura. I remember he asked his personal assistant, "Have you seen the letter-opener?" and she replied, "It's his day off." I was impressed.'

Flying the flag

A bloke called Tim See recounts how incredibly pumped up he was to see a couple of Aussies parading the national flag in front of the Barmy Army at the SCG, until ... a thousand Poms started singing (to the tune of *Bread of Heaven*) ... 'Get your shit stars off our flag!'

Tim confessed: 'I had to admit there really was no comeback.'

And nor would you think there was, but a subsequent letter from Daniel Joe Bonington recounted a beauty:

'Australian humour,' DJB pointed out, 'is that of the wry one-liner, as I, an Englishman, discovered at the Olympic Games. Responding to the jingoistic fervour that gripped the nation, I was waving my Union Jack merrily (if not in vain, Britain won no golds that night). An Aussie bloke behind me tapped me on the shoulder and with a smile said, "Hey mate, couldn't you afford the rest of the flag?"'

———

'I love your flag,' Jerry Seinfeld said, during one of his visits here. 'Britain, at night!'

Royal male

All Blacks winger Eric Rush once told me his reaction when he met the Queen of England for the first time, at Buckingham Palace on the 1990 All Blacks tour of Britain.

Growing up in New Zealand, the image of the Queen was so ubiquitous on the stamp of every letter Eric ever saw that when he met her, 'I wasn't sure whether to shake her hand or lick her on the back of the head.'

—

'Thank you, your Majesty. I voted for you.' This is what the Most Valuable Player of the 1999 World Cup, Tim Horan, said when shaking hands with the Queen after the trophy was handed over.

The game they play in heaven

A rugby referee dies and goes to heaven. Stopped by St Peter at the gates, he is told that only brave people who had performed heroic deeds and had the courage of their convictions could enter. If the ref could describe a situation in his life where he had shown these characteristics, he would be allowed in.

'Well,' said the ref, 'I was reffing a game between Australia and New Zealand in the decisive Bledisloe Cup match. The Wallabies were 1 point ahead, two minutes to go. Jeff Wilson made a break, passed inside to Josh Kronfeld. Kronfeld was driven on by his forwards, passed out to Jonah Lomu, who ducked blind and went over in the corner. However, Lomu dropped the ball before he could ground it and, as New Zealand were clearly the better side all game, I ruled that he had dropped the ball down, not forward, and awarded the try.'

'OK, that was fairly brave of you, but I will have to check it in the book,' said Peter, and disappeared to look it up. When he came back he said, 'Sorry, there is no record of this. Can you help me to trace it? When did all this happen?'

The ref looks at his watch and replies '45 seconds ago'.

Sweet revenge

As everyone knows, after decades of Test match dominance, Australian cricket has struggled during the last decade. The 2013 Ashes loss in England was particularly galling and the Poms had considerable fun at our expense:

Q. What do you call an Aussie with a bottle of champagne?
A. A waiter.

Q. What do you call a world-class Australian cricketer?
A. Retired.

Q. What do you call an Australian who can hold a catch?
A. A fisherman.

Q. Why can no one drink wine in Australia at the moment?
A. They haven't got any openers.

Q. What is the difference between Cinderella and the Aussies?
A. Cinderella knew when to leave the ball.

Q. What does an Australian batting in The Ashes have in common with Michael Jackson?
A. They both wore gloves for no apparent reason.

Q. What's the height of optimism?
A. An Aussie batsman putting on sunscreen.

Q. What's the difference between Michael Clarke and a funeral director?
A. A funeral director doesn't keep losing the ashes.

Drugs in sports

A farmer needs to buy a bull to service his cows, but has to borrow the money from the bank. The banker who lent the money comes by a week later to see how his investment is doing. The farmer complains that the bull just eats grass and won't even look at the cows. The banker suggests that a veterinarian have a look at the bull.

The next week, the banker returns to see if the vet helped. The farmer looks very pleased: 'The bull serviced all my cows twice, broke through the fence and serviced all my neighbour's cows three times.'

'Wow,' says the banker. 'What did the vet do to that bull?'

'Just gave him some pills,' replies the farmer.

'What kind of pills?' asks the banker.

'I don't know,' says the farmer, earnestly, 'but they sort of taste like chocolate.'

Size matters

At Sydney University, the rugby union players are somewhat of celebrities. After every game the players hang out at the local and enjoy hanging out with their fans, especially the female ones.

One girl liked the look of the new second-rower. Not only was he tall and good looking, but he was studying medicine!

'Hiya, big boy,' she said to him before looking his 6ft 9in frame over closely from head to toe.

'Tell me, are you built in proportion all over?'

Without skipping a beat he replied:

'If I was built in proportion, I'd be 12 ft 5.'

How wonderful

A Wallaby rugby fan is touring America on holiday and stops in a remote bar in upstate New York. He's chatting to the barman when he sees an old native American sitting in a corner, complete with full tribal gear, long plaits and wrinkles.

'Who's he?' inquires the fan.

'That's the Memory Man,' responds the barman. 'He knows everything. He can remember any sporting fact. Go and try him out.'

So the fan wanders over and asks, 'Who won the 1999 World Cup?'

'Australia,' replies the Memory Man.

The Wallaby fan is flabbergasted.

'Who scored the winning try?'

'Toutai Kefu' is the reply.

'And the score?'

'29-26.'

The Wallaby fan can't believe this and tells all his family and friends.

Five years later he is going to the States on a business trip. He decides to go back to the bar and visit the Memory Man. He finds him in the exact same spot, as if he hasn't moved in five years. He steps forward, bows and greets the old Indian in his traditional native tongue, 'How!'

The Memory Man squints and says: 'First phase after a line-out. Inside ball from Stephen Larkham.'

That's a great look you've got happening. Jockey clothes for big people.com

Medicine man

A medical professor has just finished a lecture on the subject of mental health and starts to give an oral quiz to the first years.

Speaking specifically about manic depression, the senior doctor asks, 'How would you diagnose a patient who walks back and forth, screaming at the top of his lungs one minute, then sitting in a chair weeping uncontrollably the next?'

A young man in the rear of the room raises his hand and answers: 'An NRL coach?'

———

Q. What has 26 legs and can't, for the life of it, climb a ladder?
A. Cronulla.

Quick quiz

Q: What's the difference between the Fremantle Dockers and a bra?
A: A bra has two cups, and plenty of support.

Q: What do you get when you have 34 Collingwood supporters in the same room?
A: A full set of teeth.

Q: Two Collingwood supporters jump off a cliff. Who wins?
A: Society.

Advanced English

The Victorian Shield side signs a Pakistani teenager to play in their squad. In his first training session, the coach spends half an hour explaining the game.

He points at a cricket ball and says, 'Ball.' He points at the nearby stumps and says, 'Stumps.' Then he picks up the ball and bowls it and said, 'Bowl.'

The Pakistani boy stands up, offended, and says, 'Excuse me coach, but my English is good!'

The coach responds, 'Sit down, boy. I'm talking to Merv.'

Timing is everything

There was a man named George who got a new job. His fellow employees always met for a round of golf every Saturday. They asked George to meet them at 10 am Saturdays. George replied that he would love to meet them, but he may be ten minutes late.

On Saturday morning George was there at exactly 10 am. He golfed right handed and won the round.

Next Saturday rolls around, and George says that he will be there, but he may be ten minutes late again. He shows up right on time, golfs left handed, and wins the round.

This continues for the next few weeks, with George always saying that he may be ten minutes late, and then always winning the round of golf, either left or right handed. The other employees are getting tired of this, and decide to ask him what the deal is. They say, 'George, every Saturday you say you may be ten minutes late. You never are. Then you show up and golf either right handed or left handed, and always win. What is that all about?'

George replies, 'Well, I am a very superstitious kind of guy. Every Saturday when I wake up, I look over at my wife. If she is sleeping on her left side, I golf left handed. If she is sleeping on her right side, I golf right handed.'

'Well,' one of his work mates asks, 'What happens if she is lying on her back?'

George replies, 'Then I am ten minutes late.'

Epic struggle

The Bledisloe Test of October 2013 was famously the first time that the two ace fullbacks Izzy Folau and Israel Dagg faced off against each other. The following exchange appeared in the comments section of *The Guardian*'s coverage of that Test:

Ladrone: 'When was the last time two No. 15s named Israel started a Test match?'

Jno50: 'Canaan v. Phoenicia 47BC'.

Ruggerz: 'Was that the game played in heaven?'

Jno50: 'Nah, the SPQR Stadium of Light. It was a warm-up for a Lions match (v. Christians).'

Phone a friend

Several players are in the dressing room of a well-known AFL club after a hard-fought game.

A mobile phone on a bench rings and a man engages the hands-free speaker function and begins to talk. Everyone else stops to listen.

Man: 'Hello'

Woman: 'Hi, darling, it's me. Are you still changing?'

Man: 'Yes.'

Woman: 'I'm at the shops now and found this beautiful leather coat. It's only $2,000. Is it OK if I buy it?'

Man: 'Sure, go ahead if you like it that much.'

Woman: 'I also stopped by the Lexus dealership and saw the new models. I saw one I really liked.'

Man: 'How much?'

Woman: '$150,000.'

Man: 'OK, but for that price I want it with all the options.'

Woman: 'Great! Oh, and one more thing. I was just talking to Susan and found out that the house I wanted last year is back on the market. They're asking five and a half million for it.'

Man: 'Well, then go ahead and make an offer. They'll probably take it. If not, we can go the extra hundred-thousand if it's what you really want.'

Woman: 'OK. I'll see you later! I love you so much!'

Man: 'Bye! I love you, too.'

The man hangs up.

The other men in the locker room are staring at him in astonishment, mouths wide open. They had no idea he was that well off.

He turns and asks, 'Anyone know whose phone this is?'

Cricket's curve ball

This story goes back to the mid-1930s, when the Australian cricket team, captained by the grandfather of the Chappells, Vic Richardson, was touring South Africa. Now, as Richardson was also captain of the Australian baseball team, his contacts with that sport were strong.

At the end of the tour, Richardson was instrumental in organising a charity baseball match between the baggy greens and the South African baseball side to raise funds for the widow of the late South African wicketkeeper Jock Cameron, who had died a few months earlier. And the Australians won!

The hero of the piece, however, was Stan McCabe who, after throwing away his glove as he found it easier to field that way, also hit three home runs.

When Richardson expressed his amazement at McCabe's success as a baseball batter, McCabe replied nonchalantly, 'It's easy—they were all full tosses …'

Sheer relief

One of Channel Seven's veteran cameramen, Max Davies, was right above David Besnard's fiery crash at the Bathurst 1000, and was sprayed with debris, including petrol.

He is, understandably, extremely shaken up by his near escape, and is asked by his alarmed director, 'Would you like to be relieved?'

'Don't worry,' Davies replies quietly, 'I just relieved myself.'

That explains it

In their book, *Everything a Girl Needs to Know About Football*, Simeon De La Torre and Sophie Brown describe soccer's offside rule in this easy-to-understand way:

Picture this: you're in a shoe store, second in the line. Behind the shop assistant on the counter is a pair of shoes which you have seen and which you must have. The female shopper in front of you has seen them also and is eyeing them. Both of you, however, have forgotten your purses.

It would be totally rude to push in front of the first woman if you had no money to pay for the shoes.

Your friend is trying on another pair of shoes at the back of the shop and sees your dilemma. She prepares to throw her purse to you. If she does so, you can catch the purse, then walk round the other shopper and buy the shoes. At a pinch she could throw the purse ahead of the other shopper and, whilst it is in flight, you could nip around the other shopper, catch the purse and buy the shoes.

Always remembering that, until the purse had actually been thrown, it would be plain wrong to push in front of the other shopper.

Mixed pairs

Two men nip out to the golf course for a quick nine after work. They get to the tee and see two ladies playing ahead of them. One of the men complains that the ladies will slow them down and says he is going to ask if they can play through.

He goes halfway to the ladies and turns back. The other man asks what's wrong. The man says, 'I can't go up there. That's my wife and my mistress.'

So the other man says he will go.

He goes halfway and comes back. His partner asks what happened and the man replies, 'Small world, huh?'

An engineer, doctor and priest golfing

A priest, a doctor and an engineer are waiting one morning for a particularly slow group of golfers.

Engineer: 'What's with these guys? We must have been waiting for fifteen minutes!'

Doctor: 'I don't know, but I've never seen such ineptitude!'

Priest: 'Well here comes the greens keeper. Let's have a word with him. [dramatic pause] Hi, George. What's the problem with that group ahead of us—they're rather slow, aren't they?'

George: 'Oh, yes, that's a group of blind fire fighters. They lost their sight saving our clubhouse from a fire last year, so we always let them play for free anytime.'

The group is silent for a moment.

Priest: 'That's so sad. I will say a special prayer for them tonight.'

Doctor: 'Good idea. I'll get in touch with an ophthalmologist mate of mine and see if there's anything he can do for them.'

Engineer: 'Why can't these guys play at night?'

Five-ring circus

Three guys from the bush headed to Sydney for the Olympics but they haven't got tickets.

The first picks up a manhole-cover, tucks it under his arm and walks to the gate. 'McTavish, Scotland,' he says. 'Discus.' And in he walks.

The second picks up a length of scaffolding and slings it over his shoulder. 'Waddington-Smythe, England,' he says. 'Pole vault.' And in he walks.

The third bushie looks around, picks up a roll of barbed wire and tucks it under his arm. 'O'Malley, Ireland,' he says. 'Fencing.'

We're synchronised swimmers... and we're running late!

Reg

Doing words

Some clever writing from Harry Pearson of *The Guardian*:

'It has been all bubbling exuberance at the World Athletics Championships in Daegu. Records have been broken, races have been dedicated, dreams have been dreamed, starts have been falsed and nouns have been verbed. In the last case, we should expect nothing less. Track and field leads the world in the important business of converting lumpy, dull old "naming words" into dynamic and vibrant "doing words" (a contrast with football, which has brought us nothing recently but the sullenly passive "an assist"). Vocab-wise, medalling and PB-ing are now totally part-and-parcelled, and most experts in South Korea believe podiumed, finalled and all-comered are not far off lexiconing.'

Shame on Shark

When Greg Norman and Chrissie Evert split in 2009 the *Washington Times*'s Dan Daly pointed out that Evert has now been married to an Australian, a Brit (John Lloyd) and an American (Andy Mill): 'This puts her only a Frenchman away from the matrimonial grand slam ...'

For his part, ESPN's Greg Hardy pondered how Norman and Evert will split their assets. 'Oddest thing about the split of these 54-year-olds: he keeps the tennis racquets, she gets the golf clubs ...'

Batting it back

When Jimmy Ormond walked out onto the international arena for the first time, he was told by Mark Waugh that he wasn't good enough to bat for England.

'Maybe not,' he replied. 'But at least I'm the best bat in my family.'

Slayed by a sledge

This one's from a Jason Akermanis column in *The Courier-Mail*.

Apparently, way back when Brett Voss played for St Kilda, he was lining up for a critical goal late in a game against Brisbane. He was being marked by his elder brother Michael.

Just as Brett had composed himself and was about to start his run, the elder Voss piped up: 'My dad's slept with your mum!'

It was true. It was undeniable. And Brett missed.

Mats entertainment

Former World No. 1 tennis player Mats Wilander told *The Guardian* the following joke:

A duck waddles into a bar, goes up to the barman and asks: 'Got any bread?'

Barman: 'No, sorry, we only sell drinks here.'

Duck: 'Got any bread?'

Barman: 'No, like I said, all we have is beer.'

Duck: 'Got any bread?'

Barman: 'No, I told you, WE ONLY HAVE BEER.'

Duck: 'Got any bread?'

Barman: 'FOR F**k'S SAKE, WE ONLY HAVE BEER AND IF YOU ASK ME FOR BREAD ONE MORE TIME I'M GOING TO NAIL YOUR F***ing BEAK TO THE COUNTER!!'

Duck: 'Got any nails?'

Barman: 'NO!'

Duck: 'Good. Got any bread?'

Keep walking

At a local derby between Sydney FC and Western Sydney Wanderers, a spectator suddenly finds himself in the thick of dozens of flying bottles.

'There's nothing to worry about, lad,' said the elderly English chap standing next to him. 'It's like the bombs during the war. You won't get hit unless the bottle's got your name on it.'

'That's just what I'm worried about,' says the fan. 'My name's Johnny Walker.'

Dodemaide

Many years ago, reader Dave Hurst was listening to an ABC cricket broadcast, when someone rang up to ask about the derivation of the name 'Dodemaide' as in Tony Dodemaide, the Victorian all-rounder.

Without the slightest pause, Trevor Bailey explained: 'That's an old West Indian name from the plantation days. The owner of the plantation says to his wife in regards to buying Christmas presents for the staff: "You do de butler, and I'll do de maid".'

As Hurst recalls it, co-commentator Norm O'Neill couldn't speak for five minutes and was still cracking up with laughter three or four overs later. As you would.

Golf—below par?

After a particularly bad round of golf, Robert decides not to go to the nineteenth hole and starts to go straight home.

As he is walking to the golf car park to get his Range Rover, a policeman stops him and asks, 'Did you tee off on the seventeenth hole about twenty minutes ago?'

'Yes', Robert answers.

'Did you happen to slice your ball so that it went over the trees and out of bounds and completely off the golf course?'

'Yes, I did. How did you know?' Robert questions.

'Well', said the policeman gravely, 'your golf ball flew out onto the main road and crashed through the windscreen of a BMW. The car driver lost control and crashed into six other cars and a fire engine on its way to a fire. The fire engine was unable to reach the fire it was going to in time and so the building burned down. Now, what do you intend to do about it?'

Robert thinks it over very thoughtfully and replies, 'I think I'll close my stance a little bit, tighten my grip and lower my right thumb.'

Rugger riddles

Q: Why do union players hang around in threes?
A: One can read, one can write and the other one just likes to hang around intelligent people.

Q: How can you tell if a union player has a very high IQ?
A: He is the one who can count to 21 without pulling down his pants.

Q. Why is rugby the game they play in heaven?
A. So everybody in hell has to watch it.

Q. Why do rugby wingers score so many tries?
A. Because they are marked by other rugby wingers.

Wheely good

When the great cyclist Robbie McEwen retired, I set my readers a poser: Footballers hang up their boots, but what do cyclists do?

Their brilliant responses included:

They lets the air out of their tyres.

They retyre.

They put away the chafing cream.

They hang up their Lycra.

They pull the chain.

They throw the kickstand down.

They hang up their leg razor.

They say goodbye-cycle.

They put their bikes in the rack.

Of course, when other cyclists, *far* removed from Australia, retire, they 'close the medicine cabinet'.

Daydream Island

A retired corporate executive, now a widower, decided to take a holiday. He booked himself on a Pacific cruise and proceeded to have the time of his life: that is, until the ship sank. Then he found himself on an island with no other people, no supplies, nothing; only bananas and coconuts.

After about four months, he is lying on the beach one day when the most gorgeous woman he has ever seen rows up to the shore. In disbelief, he asks, 'Where did you come from?'

She replies, 'I rowed from the other side of the island, where I landed when my cruise ship sank. I made this boat out of raw material I found there. I whittled the oars and wove the bottom from palm branches.'

'But, where did you get the tools?'

'Oh, that was no problem,' replied the woman. 'I found some alluvial rock, which I used to make some tools.'

The guy is stunned.

'Let's row over to my place,' she says.

After a few minutes of rowing, she docks the boat at a small wharf. Before him is a stone walk leading to an exquisite bungalow painted in blue and white. 'It's not much,' she says, 'but I call it home. Would you like a drink?'

'No! No, thank you,' he blurts out, still dazed. 'I can't take another drop of coconut juice.'

'It's not coconut juice,' winks the woman. 'I have a still.'

They sit down on her couch and exchange their stories. After a while she announces, 'I'm going to slip into something more comfortable. Would you like to take a shower and shave? There's a tortoise-shell razor I made upstairs in the bathroom cabinet.'

When he returns, she greets him wearing nothing but vines, strategically positioned, and smelling faintly of gardenias. She beckons for him to sit down next to her.

'Tell me,' she begins suggestively, slithering closer to him, 'we've been out here for many months. You've been lonely. There's something I'm sure you really feel like doing right now, something you've been longing for?' She stares into his eyes.

He can't believe what he's hearing.

'You mean ...' he swallows excitedly and tears start to form in his eyes. 'Don't tell me you've built a golf course!!!'

Ineffable coach takes the P

The scene was set at the Bondi Icebergs last weekend.

The coach of the Trinity First XV, Ben Morrisey, is giving a spirited address to his adoring team during pre-season training.

'Boys, the key to any game of rugby is just one word. You know what that one word is? It starts with an "F".'

No response from the team, who look at each other blankly.

'*Phases*. Phases of play is the key to any game of rugby.'

Winger (of course): 'That starts with a "P", coach.'

We're told Morrisey was probably joking.

Hits 'n' giggles

As already noted, I have long been a great admirer of the commentary work of the great Dennis Cometti, but I was sent some of the best quotes of Northern Ireland golf commentator Dave Feherty and I think he runs Our Dennis close:

'Fortunately, Rory is 22 years old so his right wrist should be the strongest muscle in his body.'

'That ball is so far left, Lassie couldn't find it if it was wrapped in bacon.'

'I am sorry Nick Faldo couldn't be here this week. He is attending the birth of his next wife.'

Jim Furyk's swing 'looks like an octopus falling out of a tree'.

'Watching Phil Mickelson play golf is like watching a drunk chasing a balloon near the edge of a cliff.'

'That green appears smaller than a pygmy's nipple.'

Umpire strikes back

In the early 1980s, Imran Khan is having a chat with an Australian player about the strength of their respective sides.

Imran says, 'Give me Sunil Gavaskar and Kapil Dev from India, and we will beat Australia.'

The laconic Australian replies, 'Imran, just give me two umpires from Pakistan and we will beat the whole world.'

Flying high

In the 1970s, the late great Muhammad Ali is flying back to the States. The flight attendant comes by and asks him to buckle his seatbelt.

He replies, 'Superman don't need no seatbelt.'

She responds, 'Superman don't need no airplane.'

A good walk spoilt

During a physical examination up Darwin way, a doctor asks a notably fit and robust retired woman about her physical activity level.

'I spend three days a week, every week in the outdoors,' she replies. 'Yesterday afternoon was typical. I took a five-hour walk about seven miles through some pretty rough terrain. I waded along the edge of a lake. I pushed my way through two kilometres of brambles. I got sand in my shoes and my eyes. I barely avoided stepping on a snake. I climbed several rocky hills. I went to the bathroom behind some big trees. I ran away from an irate crocodile then ran away from one angry bull. The mental stress of it all left me shattered. At the end of it all I drank a scotch and three glasses of wine.'

Amazed by the story, the doctor said, 'You must be one hell of an outdoor woman!'

'No,' the woman replied, 'I'm just a really, really poor golfer!'

Lost in translation

When there weren't a lot of Asian golfers in the 1970s, Japan's Isao Aoki was very much the trailblazer. Wherever he went, the press wanted to speak to him.

Unfortunately, his English was not quite as good as his golf, and an interpreter had to be called in to translate his comments to the gathered press corps. Straight-faced and meticulously, the interpreter put each question to Aoki in Japanese, then translated his replies back into English for media consumption.

The question-and-answer session was nearing a close when one hack urged the interpreter: 'Would you ask Mr Aoki how he came to drop a shot at the 11th?' This time, Aoki himself moved up to the microphone and in English announced slowly: 'I flee putt flom flucking flinge of gleen.'

Ignoring the roars of laughter ringing around the press tent, the expressionless interpreter took over again and confirmed: 'Mr Aoki says he flee putt flom flucking flinge of gleen.'

The small white ball on
the green stops twice
on its journey to the hole.
Fluck!

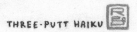

THREE-PUTT HAIKU

New ball game

Before the days of QF1, waking up in Sydney and going to bed the same day in London, it took weeks to get from Australia to England and vice versa.

Heading out for the 1962–63 Ashes, the England cricket team stopped in Aden. At a dinner party, they were introduced to a sheikh whose proud boast was that he had 81 wives.

When this was pointed out to Fred Trueman, the fast bowler quipped: 'Does he know that with four more he can have a new ball?'

Talking to a stranger

Down Caringbah way, a man enters a bar and orders a drink. Now, this particular bar has a robot barman. The robot serves him a perfectly prepared cocktail, and then asks him: 'What's your IQ?'

The man replies, '150', and the robot proceeds to make conversation about Quantum physics, environmental interconnectedness, string theory and nanotechnology.

Hugely impressed, the amazed customer decides to explore this phenomenon further. So he walks out of the bar and then a few minutes later comes back in for another drink. Again, the robot serves him the perfectly prepared drink and asks him: 'What's your IQ?'

The man responds: 'About 100.' Immediately the robot starts talking about how well he thinks Malcolm Turnbull will go, how much he loves Holden cars, the new Big Mac, tattoos and Britney Spears.

Really impressed, the man leaves the bar and decides to give the robot one more test. He heads out and returns, the robot serves him and asks: 'What's your IQ?'

The man replies: 'Err, 50, I think.' And the robot says ... really slowly: 'So ... ya gonna follow the Dragons again next year?'

First impression

The new coach comes into the club determined to turn things around. To change the culture on field and also off field.

In an attempt to prove himself to his new staff, he looks around the office and sees a guy leaning against a wall doing nothing. He approaches the guy and asks him, 'What do you think you're doing?'

The man replies, 'I'm just killing time, waiting to get paid.'

The coach is furious, 'What do you make a week?'

The man tells him, 'About $300 a week.'

The coach pulls out his wallet and hands the man $600 and says, 'There's your two weeks. Now get out of here!'

After the man leaves, the coach turns to his staff and says, 'I will not tolerate this kind of behaviour. Do any of you have anything to say about this?'

One of the staff stands up and says, 'I think he just got the largest tip he's ever gotten on a single pizza.'

Some big questions

Q. Name a major global sport. Four letters. Starts with a T.
A. Golf.

Q. Why do they call golf 'golf'?
A. Because all the other four-letter words were taken.

Q. Why is Queensland beer called 'XXXX'?
A. Because Queenslanders can't spell.

Gold medal beer

At the Olympic Games the press love to hang out and, when they do, things can get a bit parochial.

Bruce, the Aussie journo from the *Sydney Morning Herald*, shouts to the barman: 'In 'Straya, we make the best bloody beer in the world, so pour me a bloody Fosters, mate.'

Bob, from the *New York Times*, calls out next: 'In the States, we brew the finest beers in the world, and I want the king of them all. Gimme a Bud.'

Hans from *Die Welt* steps up next: 'In Germany ve invented das beer, verdamt. Give me ein Becks, ya ist der real King of Beers, *danke*.'

Then, finally, Paddy, from the *Irish Times*, steps forward: 'Barman, would ya give me a doyet coke wid ice and lemon. Tanks.'

The others stare at him in stunned silence, amazement written all over their faces. Eventually Bruce asks, 'Are you not going to have a Guinness, Pat?'

Paddy replies: 'Well, if you fookin' soft boys aren't drinkin', then neither am I.'

Seeing red

A Queensland Red goes to the team doctor the day after a gruelling game.

Doctor: 'What's wrong?'

Player: 'When I touch my legs, my arms, my head, my stomach and everywhere else it really hurts.'

Doctor: 'You've broken your finger.'

Knockout humour

Former heavyweight champion George Foreman, explaining why he called his five sons George. 'I knew that if I was going to be a successful boxer, I might suffer from memory loss.'

From Barry Michael, 57, former Australian boxing champion: 'My head has taken more hits than Google.'

Bill Simmons of ESPN Magazine on a mooted *Rocky VI* film with Sylvester Stallone: 'What could possibly be the premise? Rocky fights someone who keeps taunting him at bingo games?'

'Life is not easy. If it was easy, everyone would be doing it.' Former world champion boxer Frank Bruno.

Canadian boxer Eric Lucas, when asked whether he was superstitious or not: 'No, if you have superstitions, that's bad luck.'

Knockout humour

Dying wish

The old club president is dying, having spent his entire life pinching pennies and clinging to all of his money. Friendless, he is surrounded by the club's coach, a board member, and the club doctor.

Just before he dies he tells them, 'I know most people say that you can't bring money with you after you die, but I want you to all throw this into my grave just as they are about to bury me.' With that he hands to them three envelopes, each containing $50,000.

After his funeral the three are discussing the money. The doctor says, 'I have to confess something. I've really been wanting a vacation, so I only threw $40,000 in.'

The board member follows, 'I must also confess. We are reno-vating the kitchen, so I only threw in $25,000. I feel terrible.'

The coach lashes out at them, 'You guys are terrible! Not only did I throw in the $50,000 he gave me, but I added my own $10,000.'

The doctor is amazed, 'Why in the world would you give that greedy man your money?'

The coach replies, 'He was a good man, so I wrote him out a cheque for the full amount.'

Tunnel of lust

Travelling in a train are a Wallaby, an All Black, a blonde woman and an older lady. After several minutes of the trip, the train happens to pass through a dark tunnel, and the unmistakable sound of a slap is heard. When they leave the tunnel, the Wallaby has a big red slap mark on his cheek.

1. The blonde thinks—'That horrible Wallaby wanted to touch me and by mistake, he must have put his hand on the lady, who in turn must have slapped his face.'

2. The older lady thinks—'That dirty Wallaby laid his hands on the blonde and she smacked him.'

3. The All Black thinks—'That bloody Wallaby put his hand on that blonde and by mistake she slapped me.'

4. The Wallaby thinks—'I hope there's another tunnel soon so I can smack that stupid All Black again.'

Acting champions

During a tense London derby between Arsenal and Tottenham Hotspur at Highbury in the late 1970s, Justin Coleman, now of Leura, was then just a lad. But he remembers clearly the moment when a Spurs attacker was strongly tackled on the edge of the box and lay writhing in the customary fashion to gain sympathy.

'The crowd was hushed,' he recounts, 'waiting to see if the ref would bring out a yellow or red card, until a lone cockney voice yelled out (from a few rows behind me): "Oi! Don't bleed on our pitch!"'

———

Q: What's the difference between a football World Cup qualifier and the Academy Awards?
A: One is a group of pretty people putting on extraordinary acting performances in front of a camera in the hope of winning a little gold statue; the other is a film awards ceremony.

———

Actor Geoffrey Rush: 'When I saw the boys running towards me in rugby league, I ran the other way and never looked back. This eventually led to the opening of an envelope in Los Angeles and winning an Oscar. So I'd like to thank the entire sporting fraternity for turning me towards my career.'

Gone fishing

Beside a beautiful lake a fisheries inspector stopped a bushie carrying two eskies full of fish and asked him whether he had a fishing licence.

'No, I don't,' replied the bushie. 'But you must understand that these are my pet fish.'

'Pet fish?'

'Yeah. Every night, I take these fish down to the lake and let 'em swim 'round for a while. Then, when I whistle, they jump right back into my eskies and I take 'em home.'

'Fish can't do that!'

The bushie looked at the inspector for a moment and then said, 'It's the truth and I'll show ya. It really works.'

'OK,' said the inspector. 'I've got to see this!'

The bushie poured the fish into the lake and stood and waited.

After several minutes, the inspector says, 'Well?'

'Well, what?' asks the bushie.

The inspector says, 'When are you going to call them back?'

'Call who back?'

Ethics class

One of my readers sent me the following very interesting ethical dilemma:

Say you're playing in the club championship tournament finals and the match is tied at the end of 17 holes. Say you hit your ball 250 metres to the middle of the fairway, while your opponent then hits his ball deep into the woods. Being the gentleman you are, you help your opponent look for his ball.

Just before the permitted five-minute search period ends, your opponent says: 'Go ahead and hit your second shot, and, if I don't find it in time, I'll concede the match.'

So you hit your ball, landing it on the green about three metres from the pin. At about just the same time as your ball comes to rest, you hear your opponent exclaim from deep in the woods: 'I found it!'

The second sound you hear is a click, the sound of a club striking a ball, even as the ball comes sailing out of the woods and lands on the green, stopping no more than twenty centimetres from the hole.

Now here is the ethical dilemma: Do you pull the cheating bastard's ball out of your pocket and confront him with it, or do you keep your mouth shut?

Dyer tribe

As near as I can work it out, Jack Dyer was to Aussie Rules people in Melbourne what Rex Mossop was to us Sydney-siders—a beloved football commentator who was frequently seen to give the English language a thrashing from which it always took some time to recover.

Some of his best 'Dyerisms' are contained in a book by Paula Hunt and former AFL player Glenn Manton called *Mongrel Punts and Hard Ball Gets: An A–Z of Footy Speak*. Take it away, Jack:

'Things aren't the same now there are five teams in the four.'

'An Essendon supporter is a Collingwood supporter who can read and write.'

'Mark Lee's long arms reaching out like giant testicles.'

'I want you to pair off in threes.'

'That's the beauty of being small—your hands are close to your feet.'

So hot, it sizzles . . .

It seems that Little Johnny kept asking his dad for a television in his bedroom, to which his dad kept saying, quite reasonably, 'No.' Anyways, after all the nagging, the dad finally agrees and says, 'OK, Johnny.'

Then, several nights later, Johnny comes downstairs and asks, 'Dad, what's love-juice?'

Dad is horrified and, after looking at mum, who's also gobsmacked, he proceeds to give his son the whole works, warts and all.

Johnny now sits on the sofa with his mouth open in amazement.

Dad asks: 'So, what is it you've been watching then, son?'

Johnny replies: 'Wimbledon.'

Wisdom of the flanelled fools

Kerry O'Keeffe speaking at a function in Auckland on his first overseas trip since he retired: 'I retired in 1981 with the dream of making my living as an ABC commentator and as an after-dinner speaker. It is now 23 years later and I have been living that dream for the last three years. Anyone can have a couple of off decades.'

An unnamed cricketer talking about Shane Warne: 'We've all got skeletons in our closet, but he is deadset Rookwood.'

Judith Morris once asked her husband, Arthur, the great Test cricketer, why the gates at the SCG were named after him. He replied: 'Because I was an opener.'

Wallaby halfback v. Dublin bouncers

Nick Farr-Jones tried to enter a Dublin night-club in 1984. The bouncers said, alas, Nick couldn't come in without a tie on.

Nick fumed, he fulminated, he remonstrated. Nothing would convince them.

So he went back outside, borrowed a set of jumper leads from a taxi driver, tied them around his neck and tried again.

'What about NOW?' he asked.

'Alright …' they said, eyeing him dubiously, 'but don't try and be starting anything.'

Five-ringed circus

A man is out shopping and discovers a new brand of Olympic condoms. Clearly impressed, he buys a pack.

Upon getting home he announces to his wife the purchase he just made.

'Olympic condoms?' she blurts. 'What makes them so special?'

'There are three colours,' he replies, 'Gold, silver and bronze.'

'What colour are you going to wear tonight?' she asks cheekily.

'Gold, of course,' says the man proudly.

The wife replies, 'Why don't you wear silver? It would be nice if you came second for a change.'

A flashback to when Nasser Hussain was captain of England

Q: What's the difference between Nasser Hussain and Saddam Hussein?
A: Saddam Hussein had more victories.

Q: How bad is the English batting?
A: The selectors are thinking of moving extras up the order.

Q: What would Mark Waugh be if he was an English batsman?
A: In form.

Q: What does Alan Mullally put in his hands to make sure the next ball almost always takes a wicket?
A: A bat.

Q: What advantage do Nasser Hussain, Mark Ramprakash, Dean Headley, Alex Tudor, Alan Mullally, the Hollioakes, Mark Alleyne, Owais Shah and Graeme Hick have over the rest of their teammates?
A: At least they can say they're not really English.

A brief stopover in headline heaven

If this isn't the best sports headline in the history of the world, then I haven't seen it.

Scotland's Inverness has a soccer team named Inverness Caledonian Thistle which, because it is a bit of a mouthful, is usually shortened to Caley. Back in 2000, Caley met the legendary team Celtic in a Scottish Cup tie and, although Celtic were hot favourites to win, Caley pulled off a stunning 3-1 upset. Of course, this was big news, so you can understand that quite a bit of sports news time was devoted to reliving that glory. No less than *The Sun* newspaper ran with the headline: 'SUPER CALEY GO BALLISTIC CELTIC ARE ATROCIOUS.'

On the other hand in 2002 the Adelaide *Advertiser* came up with a headline almost as good when it reported that the captain of what England is pleased to call its 'cricket team' was close to quitting: 'THE REIGN OF HUSSAIN IS MAINLY ON THE WANE.'

A subeditor on the mighty *Byron Shire Echo* comes up with a headline for the ages after the hooker for the Mullumbimby Giants league team scored three tries against the local Marist Brothers in a 38-4 win: 'HAPPY HOOKER BLOWS PAPISTS.'

The French soccer player Eric Cantona, while playing for Manchester United, had an explosion of temper one time when he was sent off. He launched a flying kung fu kick that connected with a fan who had kept abusing him. The next day, the *News of the World* unleashed the epic headline: 'THE SHIT HITS THE FAN!'

Finally—and be warned that trying to understand this made my head hurt—there is a story that traces its origins back to a small Scottish fishing village called Bridge of Allan, which is known for harvesting tench and, more to the point, for holding annual events to see who could eat the most of this stringy fish in one sitting. It started off quite small but as it is the only contest of its kind, it soon attracted widespread, even international, contestants.

The year in question is 1990 and the final saw portly local Graham Hicks (from Fife, not far away) up against Sweden's Sven Larssen. In what was described by locals as a tough encounter, the final took place every Saturday until a best-of-five result was achieved.

Hicks ran out the eventual winner in the fourth round, eating 11 fish and beating his much fancied opponent by two.

But no one summed it up better than the local rag, *The Bridge Bugle*, which ran with the headline: 'ONE TO THREE FOR FIFE'S HICKS; SVEN ATE NINE TENCH.'

Small boy

A small boy is lost in a large shopping mall. Just barely maintaining control, he approaches a uniformed policeman and says tearfully, 'I've lost my grandpa!'

A friendly cop offers him a tissue to wipe his eyes and says, 'That's too bad. What's he like?'

The young lad hesitates for a moment, then replies, 'Bundaberg rum and bad women.'

The game of golf

Jesus and Moses are having a game of golf at the Jerusalem Golf Club, and Moses is very pleased. The old man with the flowing white hair has just hit a cracker of a drive off the fifth tee, to take his ball about five hundred and fifty natural cubits forward, and within just a stone's throw of the hole. He has every chance of making a birdie.

It is at this point that Jesus steps up and shanks the ball viciously to the left. It heads straight towards the deep forest that lies there. Just then, however, a chipmunk pops up on a branch that the ball is going to pass over and *head-butts* the ball back onto the course! Still, Jesus is not saved, as the ball now plops into a water trap. Not a split second after it has landed, though, a large fish comes from the depths and jumps high into the air with the ball in its mouth, even as an eagle swoops from nowhere, grabs the fish with the ball and starts shaking it! Five seconds later, a bolt of lightning comes from the clear blue sky, causing the eagle to drop the fish and the ball, just as they are flying over the green. The ball comes loose on impact and begins to trickle about two inches to the right of the hole. Just when it appears that it is going to miss, an earthworm comes from the ground and whips its tail around in such a fashion that the ball is diverted and falls into the hole! It is nothing less than a *hole-in-one*!

Jesus jumps around in celebration, but Moses is appalled.

Says he, looking Jesus straight in the eye, 'Do you want to play golf, or do you want to f**k around?'

Country matters

Having just spent a fortnight up on his Uncle Jed's spread in northern Victoria, young Mitch is cock-a-hoop when he gets back to his home in Malvern.

'Uncle Harold has everything,' he tells his smiling parents at the dinner table that night. 'He's got goats, chooks, sheep, pigs, bulls, cows and f**kers.'

'He's got *what*?' his parents burst out in unison.

'Well, to be fair,' says Mitch, 'Uncle Jed called them 'eifers, but I knew what he meant.'

Commentariat capers

'The event obviously has a lot of knockers, but organisers say it is just fun.' A straight-faced female reporter on Channel 10's late news, doing a story on the 'Nude Olympics' being held on a beach near Adelaide.

'She can see her competitors because she is [a] bilateral breather on both sides.' Former Olympic silver medallist Nicole Stevenson commenting on women's 200m freestyle swimmer Elka Graham.

The talented Mick Molloy, doing a spot of commentating on Channel Nine during the Commonwealth Games. 'And sadly, the women's boxing has had to be cancelled. It seems all the women lied about their weight division.'

BBC live text commentary from Wimbledon in 2009 as Lleyton Hewitt fought every breath of the way only to lose to Andy Roddick in five sets in the quarter-finals: 'I can't help thinking he was wasted playing tennis, he should have been on the *Granma* with Castro and Guevara, or drinking his own urine on the *Endeavour* with Captain Cook ...'

David Letterman, some time ago: 'America is the only country where a significant proportion of the population believes that professional wrestling is real but the moon landing was faked.'

'I once dated a famous Aussie rugby player who treated me just like a football: made a pass, played footsie, then dropped me as soon as he'd scored.' Kathy Lette

Jock gets the last laugh

A Scottish supporter attended last weekend's quarter-final between the Wallabies and the Scots in Brissie. Just as he has done in previous games he watches in full regalia kilt, sporran, the lot, as his blokes went perilously close, in the first half at least, to sending proud Eddie's Army homewards to think again.

When, however, at the end of the game, the Wobblies had taken a hard-fought win, one Australian supporter, the-life-of-the-party type, leans over and says cheerily to the devastated man: 'Hey, mate, my mum wears a dress like that.'

Morosely, shaking his head, the Scot replies: 'Aye, I know. It took me ages to get her out of it last night.'

Accept no substitutes

One of my more astute and intelligent readers in New Zealand, an Australian, dropped into a Dunedin pub on Wednesday afternoon to catch the end of the Australian innings in the one-day match. He writes:

'Adjacent to the TV showing the cricket was another showing the races. During a commercial break in the cricket, my attention turned to a greyhound race just as the dogs jumped.

The race was a typically frenetic and boring affair ... until the turn into the straight, when the leading dog plus two others came to a sudden halt, did a U-turn and hurtled off in the other direction.

The slow-mo replay revealed that a weal wive bunny wabbit had wun onto the twack. It clearly was a much more attractive option than the synthetic bugger that they were always chasing.

Race abandoned!'

Out of the mouths of jocks

From Vince Sorrenti, at a Drummoyne Water Polo lunch: 'Shane Warne—the only Madame Tussaud's figure that looks more lifelike than the real thing.'

'They yell fore, shoot six and write down five.' Golfer Chi Chi Rodriguez on playing with present and former US presidents.

'I thought you were talking about a new Mexican player that we had.' Neil Balme, the football manager of Collingwood, in response to a journalist's question concerning how morale was going.

'It must be a comedy if a British player is winning at Wimbledon!' So said Serena Williams, on hearing the news of a new film called *Wimbledon,* in which an unheralded Brit actually goes on to win the world's most prestigious tennis tournament.

Portly Parramatta Eels prop Stan Jurd was once asked what he did the 400 metres in. Stan replied: 'In me ute ...'

Olympic speed-skating gold medallist Steven Bradbury at the launch of the West Coast's 2012 AFL season. 'The only person who would have spent more time on the ice than me was Ben Cousins.'

Number one sport

A woman, while touring a small South American country was shown a bullfight.

The guide told her, 'This is our No. 1 sport.'

The horrified woman said, 'Isn't that revolting?'

'No,' the guide replied, 'revolting is our No. 2 sport.'

The buzz of recognition

One of the amazing things about touring with the Wallabies in New Zealand is the extraordinary amount of adulation you receive whenever you are recognised, which is frequent. No, we Wallabies will never be treated as demi-gods, as are the All Blacks, but we don't do a bad little line as minor deities.

For example, the other night in Christchurch I'd no sooner entered the restaurant than everybody was staring and pointing at me, whispering behind their hands and winking and smiling at me in such a friendly fashion I was almost overcome with gratitude.

This went on all through dinner. I was the centre of attention in a whole crowded restaurant of hob-nobs, and my fellow diners were in such awe of me they didn't even dare approach, however enthusiastically I waved and winked back.

Sure, there'll be folks back home who won't believe me, and will doubt that such hero-worship could happen to a footballer such as me. But just ask David Campese or Nick Farr-Jones— they were right by my side the whole time ...

The real Ashes

In the main square of Frankfurt before England's first match of the World Cup, their supporters have taken over the pubs and are singing at anyone coming by, particularly anyone wearing green and gold. This includes their latest favourite, *Where's your Ashes gone? Where's your Ashes gone!*

Now happens along a group of half a dozen happy-go-lucky young Australians. The Poms start in with their chants, expecting another capitulation. But not these little black ducks. The Australians huddle, talk and now come out swinging, singing to the tune of *She'll be coming round the mountain*. Let's sing with them!

Shane Warne's shagging all your women while you're here,
Shane Warne's shagging all your women while you're here,
Shane Warne's shagging all your women,
Shagging all your women,
Shane Warne's shagging all your women while you're here

And they've gone and sold the pictures to The Sun,
And they've gone and sold the pictures to The Sun,
They've gone and sold the pictures
Gone and sold the pictures
Yes, they've gone and sold the pictures to The Sun.

The response of the English: laughs and applause all round, mixed with lots of handshakes as the Australians move off. Not a World Cup win, but not bad.

And it makes me proud to be an Australian!

Scoreboard doesn't lie

According to BBC Sports, this was the exchange during the Kangaroos' drubbing of England, 52-4, during their 2009 tour.

Aussie league fans: 'Aussie, Aussie, Aussie; Oi, Oi, Oi!'

England fans: 'You've only got one song!'

Aussies: 'You've only got one try!'

A caddy full of jokes

Golfer: 'Think I'm going to drown myself in the lake.'
Caddy: 'Think you can keep your head down that long?'

———

Golfer: 'I'd move heaven and earth to break a hundred on this course.'
Caddy: 'Try heaven—you've already moved most of the earth.'

———

Golfer: 'Do you think I can get there with a five iron?'
Caddy: 'Eventually.'

———

Golfer: 'You've got to be the worst caddy in the world.'
Caddy: 'I don't think so, sir. That would be too much of a coincidence.'

———

Golfer: 'Please stop checking your watch all the time. It's too much of a distraction.'
Caddy: 'It's not a watch—it's a compass.'

———

Golfer: 'How do you like my game?'
Caddy: 'Very good, sir, but personally I prefer golf.'

—

Golfer: 'That can't be my ball—it's too old.'
Caddy: 'It's been a long time since we teed off, sir.'

Chaser bites Bulldog

Chas Licciardello, after a court appearance to defend a charge that he and the lads of *The Chaser* made criminal nuisances of themselves when they did a skit outside a Bulldogs game, offering to sell supporters kits including balaclavas, fake knuckle-dusters and fake knives: 'All I want to say is, it is a case of four quarters and full credit to the prosecution. I thought they did a good job. They gave as good as they got. I am really proud of our boys, they gave 110 per cent. I play tough, hard and fair and I think the results take care of themselves.'

Know names

In the beginning, there was 'Kick-Too' Farr-Jones, a nickname started off by erstwhile colleague John Huxley, and it was good, and it was great. And then there was Martin 'Chariots' Offiah, and it was even better because, from the moment someone called the rugby league player this, it was obvious that no one could ever call him anything else again.

The great Newtown fullback Phil Sigsworth was known as 'Whatsapacketa'. Steve Larkham was known as 'The Pope' on the grounds that 'he wouldn't pass the pill'. More recently there has been 'Waltzing' Matt Hilder, the leaguie who ended up playing for the Newcastle Knights.

There's the great South African fast bowler 'All Hands' Zondeki, and the famed English fast bowler Gladstone Small, who was known for being rather on the neckless side of things and was therefore affectionately known as 'Pearl'—as in Pearl neckless!

Sometimes it is commentators who give the best nicknames, a la Roy and H.G. calling rugby league prop Glenn Lazarus 'The Brick With Eyes.' In the 1980s, NSW had a highly regarded magistrate by the name of Lillian Thompson. Her nickname was—of course!—'Two Fast Bowlers'.

The ABC cricket broadcaster Neville Oliver was affectionately known by his colleagues as 'Fart-in-the-bath'. Why? Well, try saying his name quickly, over and over.

On the US PGA tour, they don't call our own Aaron Baddeley 'Badds' or 'AB' or anything like that. Instead, in honour of his rather loud fashion sense and predilection for wearing checked trousers and tight colours-of-the-rainbow shirts they're calling him ... wait for it ... 'Dresses', as in 'Dresses Baddeley'.

Petero Civoniceva was once known as 'Petrol Seventy-cents-a-litre', while a certain well-known NRL prop who retired 15 years ago was unkindly referred to as 'King Prawn'—all meat from the neck down and shit for brains.

There is the local footballer who never shouts his mates at the pub, who's known as 'Crime,' because crime doesn't pay. Up in Gosford, a soccer striker by the name of Mark Green is called 'Jigsaw' because he went through a spell where 'every time he got in the box he fell to pieces'. A Sydney jockey from the 1970s is still known as 'Autumn Leaves' as he seemed to be always falling to the ground, and a rugby coach in Perth, who was perpetually stoned on dope, was known by his players as the 'Silver Surfer ...' because he was 'always out there'. (Not a great coach, but apparently they had some amazing training sessions.) In Sydney, there is a rugby coach known as 'Sunset' because he always talked about 'at the end of the day'.

Down at the Woolgoolga surf club, meantime, when a presentation was made to a large bloke named Percival, the presenter congratulated Perce and then said: 'You're too big for a purse, we'll call you "Handbag",' and he has been that ever after, just as his little brother is 'Wallet'.

Best of all, however? That would be Billy Tait, who rowed for Australia a decade ago, and is these days a senior rowing coach. He is known by former teammates as 'Rehab', as in 'Rehab-Billy-Tait'.

Law of relativity

Einstein's Theory of Getting Kicked Out of Rugby League goes like this: the chances of any player being sacked by a club are equal to the amount the club is above the salary cap, divided by the player's ability, multiplied by the player's wage, divided again by the seriousness of the offence.

Therefore, if you are a struggling player on a high contract, you could be dumped for picking your nose in public. If, however, you are a representative player and essential to your team's success, then the minimum offence for being kicked out would be regicide. And even then you'd be a rough chance of holding on if your tackle count was high.

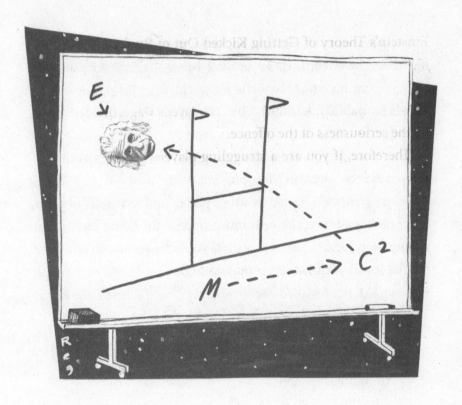

How many Dicks for a Dean?

A few years ago at a luncheon in Sydney, Sir Richard Hadlee recounted how, while down in Melbourne, he noticed a woman lining up for an autograph who looked awfully familiar.

'Hang on,' Sir Richard said, 'I'm sure I've already signed for you.'

'Yes,' she replied, 'but when I get ten of your autographs, I can swap it for one of Dean Jones's.'

Sir Richard also pulled from his pocket a dog-eared copy of a letter he'd got from a 64-year-old inmate at an Auckland prison, asking for a certain piece of Hadlee signed memorabilia.

The letter acknowledged the bloke was asking for a lot with this request, but finished encouragingly: 'PS: If it helps, the house I burgled was owned by an Australian ...'

A league of wits

After Queensland thumped NSW many seasons ago, Super Coach Jack Gibson commented: 'NSW were in this game right up until the national anthem finished.'

———

Wally Lewis nostalgically recalled: 'Les Boyd was a character. I found out a whole lot more about my wife, mother and any girlfriends I'd had after playing a game against him.'

———

Luke Rooney, the Kangaroos winger, on 2UE, after spending four miserable days in Prague with some of his teammates: 'It was boring; none of us liked it. There was nothing to do. There were hardly any pubs, no TABs. I'd rather be in Penrith ...'

Peter Sterling, commentating on a State of Origin match in which Michael Crocker was, once again, right in the middle of a melee: 'Crocker retaliated first.'

———

Channel Nine commentator Ray Warren on identical twins Brett and Josh Morris playing for Country Origin: 'The only way I can tell them apart is [Josh] has black tape around one of his boots.'

Peter Sterling, after a superbly theatrical pause: 'They're wearing different numbers, Ray.'

Vetell it like it is

Sebastian Vettel has already won the Formula One world championship four times and in interviews he ain't your usual cliche-a-thon contestant with four on the floor and overdrive button ready to flick into action at a moment's notice.

When he won his very first F1 in Italy, a journalist said to him, 'This must be the best day of your life?'

Vettel replied: 'You obviously weren't there when I lost my virginity.'

Captain Marvel

Back in the '60s the town of Sea Lake in the Mallee in Victoria had a pretty handy footy team in the Tyrell League. The heart and soul of their team was Smokey O'Toole, who doubled as the local fire captain.

Smokey was renowned for his spectacular high marks, fleetness of foot and unerring accuracy when kicking for goal. But speaking of smoke, what's that?!

In 1966, the tallest building in town—the three-storey Royal Hotel—was on fire. The local brigade was there in minutes, led of course by Smokey. Smokey was shouting out orders and getting hoses directed when the watching crowd was silenced by a deafening scream from the top floor of the burning hotel.

In a smoke-filled window, there stood pretty Moira O'Brien, screaming and holding out her young child for rescue.

Seeing no way of reaching her quickly, the nearest fireman called for her to throw the baby out to him. But she refused. He begged and pleaded, but to no avail.

Just as he was about to give up, someone in the crowd yelled, 'Go and get Smokey!!' The entire crowd picked up the shout—'Get Smokey! Get Smokey!'

The terrified Moira suddenly perked up and also joined in the chant. 'Yes, get Smokey!' she cried. 'Get Smokey—he can catch little Bridget and save her!'

Right on cue, Smokey came striding around the corner, and Moira tossed the young girl out the window.

Well, the way my informant, Shane Clohesy, tells it, our Smokey didn't miss a beat. He took three or four quick strides and flew above the shoulders of the fireman waiting below.

Hands outstretched, eyes only for the child, his boots danced lightly on the fireman's shoulders as the little one settled safely and tightly in his strong, safe hands.

The crowd roared and cheered as one as Smokey hit the ground with the tot in hand. And they roared again as he turned towards the crowd ... raced off, took two bounces and kicked her straight and true for another goal!

Media natters

On this particular afternoon the ABC Sunday afternoon sports program *The Hit-Up*, hosted by Debbie Spillane, had Mario Fenech as a panellist posing questions to Roosters coach Trent Robinson.

Fenech opens with a curly one: 'I'm only going to say one word—S.B.W.'

Spillane: 'Ah, Mario, that's three letters, not one word.'

Fenech: 'Oh OK, you got me … Jeez, you're sharp today, Deb!'

———

The *Footy Show* one Thursday night included a quiz section, with Fatty Vautin as quiz master.

Fatty: 'Which country worships the rooster symbol?'

Jamal Idris: 'Chile?'

Fatty: 'Why would you pick Chile?'

Idris: 'I don't know, chicken and chilli … they go together?

Fatty: 'I am going to make an executive decision and give you 10 points. It's Japan but I'm giving you 10!'

The whang man

One time Ian Chappell was trying to guide Jeff Thomson to a slightly more nuanced approach to taking wickets: to think about swinging the ball perhaps, or changing his rhythm to get more bounce; or setting the batsmen up with the first three balls of the over so as to try to take his wicket on the fourth, etc...

'I don't know about any of that sort of bullshit,' Thomson is said to have replied, 'I just shuffle up and go whang!'

No one has ever gone whang! like Thommo did.

Three quiz questions

My best man legally married his brother, the famous footballer. How?

In which month of the year do footballers, cricketers, netballers, golfers, hurdlers, etc. all eat the least?

No kidding, no joking, every year more people die in Australia playing one particular sport than in motor racing, sky diving, rock fishing, football and hang gliding combined. This sport was banned by an English king; but the Australian Government still allows it to be played and it is even in the Commonwealth Games. What is this Australian game with such a devastating mortality rate?

The answers

1. He was a minister and performed the marriage. So he legally 'married' his brother.

2. February, of course. It is the shortest month of the year.

3. Lawn bowls.

My best man legally married his brother, the famous Italian

Rough end of the sledge

So legend has it, the great Australian fast bowler, Dennis Lillee, used the following sledge on batsmen throughout his storied career.

Lillee: 'I can see why you are batting so badly; you've got some shit on the end of your bat.'

This would usually cause the batsman to examine the bottom of his bat.

Lillee: 'Wrong end, mate.'

BOONIE!

Rough edge sledge

Somehow or other, the aura about David Boon, the former Test batsman from Tasmania, has endured to the point that a beer company put out tens of thousands of models of the Boonie doll, capable of saying many Boon-like things when placed near a television set on which a game was being played.

The day of the first televised match in January, for example, Boonie piped up with: 'Cricket's about to start …' and 'Better grab a beer!' The doll continued to 'talk' before and during games until everyone was driven to distraction. Nevertheless, Georgie Zaikowski, home on a Chrissie break from university in Rhode Island, was so taken with it, she took it back to Rhode Island with her to add to the Australian sport shrine in her room.

Alas, her journey was a shocker: delayed flights from Sydney and LA, stranded in Cleveland overnight, and finally arriving at 9.30 am in sub-zero temperatures with a full day of classes to attend. At last, late that night, having gone for 48 hours without sleep, she dragged herself to bed and was long gone in the land of nod when the previously dormant BOONIE—no doubt having over-imbibed on the flight and himself broken all records—suddenly turned feral.

'The cricket's about to start!' he roared into the darkness, desperately trying to awaken his countrywoman to the possibilities of it all. 'The word for today is "thirsty"!'

You can take the young woman out of Australia, but you still can't take the Australian's Australian off her.

Any excuse for a joke

Here are some of the best one-liners from the famously deadpan American comedian Steven Wright. The first of them even has a vague sporting angle.

'There's a fine line between fishing and just standing on the shore like an idiot.'

'We had one of those new microwave fireplaces put in at our place,' he recounted. 'Now you can lie in front of the fire the whole night long and it only takes ten minutes.'

'Right now I'm having amnesia and deja vu at the same time. I think I've forgotten this before.'

'I almost had a psychic girlfriend but she left me before we met.'

'And here's one of the deepest philosophical questions of all time. "If a man was talking, deep in the forest, and there was no woman there to hear him, would he still be wrong?"'

The beauty of Brock

Following the death of beloved rugby figure David Brockhoff, I received many lovely reminiscences from readers about their dealings with him. Mark Kenna from Scots College at Bellevue Hill reported that, for much of the past three decades, it was almost a rite of passage for the coaches and players of the First XV to have a 'session with Brock'. Towel around his neck, tucked into his track-suit, he would unleash in classic fashion, holding the ball up for all to see, and with help from my friends, this is what he was like:

'It's in the noodle, fellas. Passed down from God himself through Moses, Danie Craven, then to Brock. The fruit boys, the FRUIT! You'll run out, you'll line up on the other side of halfway, and … no excuses, cause havoc at the breakdown like sharks in a school of mullet. And when you're through the other side we're like crowbars through the Opera House window. We get in, loot the joint and get out. Quick seed to the Dancing Man all day, fellas, all day like wind through the wheat. Centre stage, I want to see arms through the briar bushes and dinosaur steps through the guts. And boys, when we get to the top of the mountain, grand piano stuff, we plant the flag! Above all, slaughter house, Friday night fight night at the old showgrounds, blood on the floor. We must have the fruit, so every lineout a dockyard brawl. But not in our 22. There, row of ministers.'

Coaches learnt to bring him in on a Tuesday because it often took the rest of the week to explain to the players what he had said.

Easy-access mortification

I ducked into a fetish club on Thursday night, in Apple Crumble Street, Redfern.

'I want to be dominated and humiliated,' I told Madame Lash.

'That will cost you $100,' says she.

That sounds reasonable,' says I. 'What do I get for that?'

'An Australian Wallabies jersey and a green mouthguard!' says she.

Reddy-made puns

NSW opening batsman Greg Mail was a Blues stalwart ten years ago. At that time, reader Mike Reddy of the ACT called for Greg's selection for the first Test against New Zealand.

Reddy wrote: 'This has nothing to do with his 150 not out for NSW against South Australia; it's all to do with the boundless possibilities for word-play offered by his terrific surname. Apparently his team nickname is "Junk" but there is much more scope than that.

'Consider the possible headlines: Greg plays his first game for NSW: "First-class Mail." Greg goes through a form slump: "Ordinary Mail." Greg elevated up the batting list: "Mail opened." Greg dives high to take a catch: "Air Mail." Greg forgets training: "The late Mail." Greg takes up fast bowling: "Express Mail." Greg presented to the Queen at Lord's Test: "Royal Mail." Greg sent home in disgrace from Ashes series (for goosing the Queen): "Return to sender."

'Not to mention the other passing comments. Mail gives pre-match address; Mail puts his stamp on the game. And at the very end, at the Greg Mail funeral, he is carried away on the shoulders of teammates in a ... Mail box.'

Gotta love a billabonk

A reader passed on the results of something called an Ozwords competition (I don't know who invented it but they're very clever), where entrants were asked to take an Australian word, alter it by only one letter, and supply a new and witty definition. Examples: *Billabonk*: to make passionate love beside a waterhole; *Bludgie*: a partner who doesn't work but is kept as a pet; *Dodgeridoo*: an imitation indigenous artifact; *Fair drinkum*: good quality Australian wine; *Flatypus*: a native animal which has been run over by a 4WD; *Crackie daks*: hipster tracksuit pants.

Here are some more Ozwords with a sporting flavour, sent in by some pretty clever readers.

Ping Pang: Injury sustained while playing table tennis.

Cricket Pest: Any member of the Barmy Army.

Dack High: The underwear of choice for Australia's senior sporting contingency.

Linesmon: A West Indian touch judge.

Ricky Punting: The boy from Tabmania.

Squids: What anglers wouldn't be dead for.

*F**k*: Sound from the bottom of a rugby ruck.

Tanks for the memory

Former Wallaby prop Chris 'Buddha' Handy was in the back-blocks of Queensland, about to get on a light plane back to Brissie after a speaking gig.

'How much do you weigh?' the Rex Airlines person behind the counter asked.

'Why?' Buddha asked.

'We need to know how much petrol to put in the plane.'

'I'm 250 kilos! FILL IT UP!'

Putting around

Three unmarried men were waiting to tee off when the starter walked up to them and said, 'You see that beautiful blonde practising her putting?'

'Her? Wow, she is beautiful,' they all said.

'She's a good golfer,' he continued, 'and would like to hook up with a group. None of the other groups will play with a woman. Can she play with you? She won't hold you up, I promise.'

They looked at each other and said, 'Sure! She can join us.'

Just as the starter said, the woman played well and kept up. Plus, they kept noticing she was very attractive.

When they reached the 18th hole, she said that if she sank her 18-footer, she'd break 80 for the first time. 'Guys, I'm so excited about breaking 80 that I have to tell you something. I had a great time playing with you. I can tell you all really love golf. I want you to know that I'm single and want to marry a man who loves golf as much as I do. If one of you guys can read this putt correctly and I make it, I'll marry whichever of you was right!'

All three jumped at the opportunity. The first one looked over the putt and said, 'I see it breaking 25cm left to right.' The second looked it over from all sides and said, 'No, I see it breaking 20cm right to left.'

The third man looked at the woman, looked at the ball, and said, 'Pick it up. It's good!'

Quick thinker

Late one night a Waratahs fan is speeding home when a police-man pulls him over. The cop says to the fan, 'Are you aware of how fast you were going?'

The fan replies, 'Yes, I am. I'm trying to escape a robbery I got involved in.'

The cop looks shocked that the man admitted this. 'So you're telling me you were speeding ... AND committed a robbery?'

'Yes,' the fan calmly says. 'I have the loot in the back.'

The cop begins to get angry. 'Sir, I'm afraid you have to come with me.'

The cop reaches in the window to subdue the man. 'Don't do that!' the fan yells. 'I'm scared you'll find the gun in my glove box!'

The cop pulls his hand out. 'Wait here,' he says.

The cop calls for backup. Soon cops, police cars and heli-copters are flooding the area. The fan is cuffed quickly and taken towards a police car.

However, before he gets in, a cop walks up to him and says, while gesturing to the cop that pulled him over, 'Sir, this officer informed us that you had committed a robbery, had stolen goods in the boot of your car, and had a loaded gun in your glove box. However, we found none of these things in your car.'

The fan replies, 'Yeah, and I bet that liar said I was speeding too!'

Basket racket

A strip club owner in America has appeared in court, accused of paying off the Mafia and providing prostitutes for NBA players.

'Hey, the guy was just trying to help out,' comedy writer Alex Kaseberg told the *San Francisco Chronicle*. 'Everyone knows how hard it is for the Mafia to make money and for NBA players to meet women.'

Phar-fetched

A reader asked me to believe that in Australia there have actually been two racehorses with the registered names of Phar Call and Far Kinnell, while a horse ran in England called Here I Come With My Left Eye Hanging Out. 'I thought there were restrictions on the number of letters allowed in a horse's name but I swear this horse did go round, I think in the late '70s,' the reader said. Of course it did, sir. Of coooouuuurse it did! Now go and have a good lie down.

And the same goes to the reader who tried to tell me there was a racehorse called Irish Wristwatch, which actually raced long enough to cause carnage among the tongues of race callers who tried to say it quickly.

A reader by the name of Brett has sworn on the head of his mother that running last year in the Toowoomba area was a nag called Bucket of Vyno. 'When I first heard it run, as the finish approached and the race call intensified, a casual listener would have been forgiven for thinking that the race caller had forgotten the name of one of the runners.' Quite.

And finally, finally, a reader by the name of Timo swears blind that there was a horse in the States called Hoof Hearted. 'One of the major stations showed one of its races a couple of years ago, when it won. The commentary went something like this, "… and making a late charge … Hoof Hearted! Hoof Hearted! Hoof Hearted!"'

What a wipeout

Two Aussies were drinking in a Brompton Road pub, boasting about Australia's sporting prowess.

A chinless wonder heard all this and finally said, 'Look heah you chairps, it's jolly baird form to be so boastful. Airctually we Bwiddish invented all of these games and let you Johnny-come-lately fellows participate. Just give me one sport that we Bwiddish did not invent!'

Quick as a flash, Bluey from Bondi said 'What about bloody surfin'?'

'My deah fellow,' replied Peregrine, pompously, 'we had serfing long before the Magna Carta, but the serfs simply would not take to it.'

Last stop at the 19th

The death of Robert Trent Jones, regarded as 'the father of modern golf course architecture', in Florida in 2000 at the age of 93, prompted all the best stories to be retold about him.

My favourite, recounted in New Zealand's *Sunday Star*, went back to 1952, when he was under attack from the golf committee of the Baltusrol Club for designing a par three on the fourth hole that they claimed was far too difficult. In response, Jones took the entire recalcitrant committee out to the fourth, placed a ball on the pin and hit a hole-in-one.

'Gentlemen,' he said, 'I think the hole is eminently fair.' And then he walked off without another word. No further arguments.

Almost 50 years later, when the end was near, his two sons were by his side in hospital when he momentarily came out of a coma.

'Am I going to die?' he asked his oldest boy, Bobby.

'No, Dad,' Bobby replied gently. 'You've had a stroke.'

'Do I have to count it?'

The world game of shame

Fran Kelly on Radio National one Wednesday morning, talking to sports reporter Warwick Hadfield.

Kelly: 'So what chance Frank Lowy will be able to recoup the $43 million spent on the World Cup campaign from FIFA?'

Hadfield: 'Sweet FFA, I'd say …'

Michael Garcia, the newly appointed joint chief investigator of FIFA's ethics committee, has said the awarding of the 2018 and 2022 World Cups to Russia and Qatar respectively will come under scrutiny: 'If you look at things, it is clear there is something to investigate, and that is what we are going to do.'

Eat your heart out, Sherlock Holmes.

—

Q: 'FIFA's president, secretary general and communications director are all travelling in a car. Who's driving?'

A: 'The police.'

Working out

A man asks a trainer in the gym: 'I want to impress that beautiful girl over there, which machine can I use?'

The trainer replied, 'Why don't you try the ATM outside the gym!'

Signature stupidity

One of Laurie Daley's favourite yarns dates back to 1989, when Tim Sheens was coach of the Canberra Raiders. In their run-up to that year's victory in the grand-final, the Raiders played a game against Canterbury in Perth. Soon after they had landed, Sheens told them he wanted them all tucked up in bed by ten at the latest the whole time they were there.

Daley and three teammates decided to ignore the curfew and slipped out after midnight on the Thursday night. They didn't get back until well after 4am, only to find that the following day Sheens called all four of them in and gave them a dressing-down that damn nigh made their ears bleed. But how had he found out? They hadn't seen anyone from the team on the way back in and none of them had blabbed.

A fortnight after their victory over Balmain in the grand-final, Daley and the other players tackled Sheens after the main celebratory dinner. Well, Sheens replied, it was like this: after they had checked in to their Perth hotel, he had noticed the young woman on night duty at reception was exceptionally good looking. Taking her aside, he asked a favour. If any time after midnight someone came into the hotel that looked like a footballer, could she get their autograph? She agreed, and the job was done!

'Yeah,' said one of Daley's teammates, 'but anyone could have forged those signatures.'

'Yes,' said Sheens. 'But how would that person have known to scrawl the correct room-number beneath your signature?!'

And they're racing

And they're racing

Here's one of my favourite pieces of racing commentary. Please take it away Adelaide's legendary race caller Alf Gard, calling a race at Victoria Park nigh on 30 years ago:

'Down the back straight and there's one taking off from the rear ... It's absolutely flying ... The colours are obscured from my view. I can only see the white cap, but it's doing two to their one ... Never seen a horse move so fast in my life ...

'Oh ... it's a fella on a motorcycle on Fullarton Road.'

It's fun if you do the hard yards

They call it 'Football Finals Bingo', and it is growing in popularity every year. The idea is to get a group of friends together and form a list of your ten favourite commentator cliches. Then watch a football final and tick off each one as it occurs. Circulate your choice to friends, and you're ready. Shout 'Bingo!' every time you score.

'Arm wrestle.' An absolute gimme to get everyone started. Most games are 'arm wrestles' at some point.

'Not the start they were looking for.' Whenever one team scores early in any final, the commentator will wisely note that this wasn't what the opposing team had hoped would happen.

'Heavily strapped.' No one, it seems, simply has tape applied these days. All injuries are 'heavily strapped'.

'Injured in back play.' This is where all injuries seem to occur. Any player wishing to avoid injury should never venture into back play.

'The modern game.' Apparently there are many things that 'can't be done in the modern game'. For a bonus point, name the date the modern game commenced.

Coach 'looking on'. Cutaways to the coach's box will be accompanied by, for example, 'Des Hasler looking on'. It's what coaches do during games: they look on.

The siren goes off 'in the background'. Sirens never go off in the foreground, always 'the background'.

Fun for the whole family!

Wisdom of the world game

John Lambie, former manager of Scottish football club Partick Thistle, when told a concussed striker did not know who he was: 'That's great, tell him he's Pele and get him back on.'

———

Reader Garry Wheelhouse after that famous match of yesteryear: 'I'm no expert on soccer (oops, football), but why in the world did they send the Uruguayan diving team to play Australia?'

———

A club official from Peru's Deportivo Wanka soccer club on a surprising surge in UK merchandise sales, on the basis of their name: 'It is very strange. Everyone in Britain seems to think we have a funny name.'

A few good props

Paul Jurdeczka emailed me a spoof created by the lads from the Thirsty Third Grade of the Macquarie University Beacons. It is based on the famous courtroom scene in *A Few Good Men*, in which Colonel Jessup, in the person of Jack Nicholson, gives his thundering oration from the dock to Lieutenant Kaffee (Tom Cruise), justifying Marine atrocities. But here it is a prop forward giving a namby-pamby winger the rounds of the kitchen:

'Son, in this world there are scrums. And in those scrums you need props. Are you willing to do it? As a prop, I have more responsibility than you can possibly fathom. You use words like "drunk" and "out of shape"—those words are the very backbone of a life I spent drinking and partying in, and you use them as a punchline.

'You weep for your wingers and centres, and you curse the prop forward. You have that luxury. You have the luxury of not knowing what I know: that the front row, while grotesque and incomprehensible to you, wins these games you play. Truth? You can't handle the truth, because deep down, in places you don't talk about in your selection meetings, you want me in that scrum; you need me in that scrum.

'I neither have the time nor inclination to explain myself to a back who scores under the very blanket of ball retention that I provide, and then questions the manner in which I provide it. I would rather you just bought me a beer and went on your way. Otherwise, I SUGGEST YOU CRAWL INTO THAT SCRUM AND GET DIRTY.'

Come in, spinner

The scene is set on 3 January 2003, when the Australian captain, Steve Waugh, is on 98 runs at the SCG, on the last ball of the day.

Up in the ABC commentary box, England's Jonathan Agnew and Australia's Kerry O'Keefe are doing the honours, their words being beamed right around Australia and the United Kingdom.

Agnew: 'Well, what high drama we have here, Kerry. What will he do?'

O'Keefe: 'He'll go for it.'

Agnew: 'But he could come back tomorrow and wait for a trundler down the leg side …'

O'Keefe: 'Stuff tomorrow, Aggers. Tomorrow is for silver medallists. We're Australians. *Poms* come back tomorrow. Australians only want the gold and we want it now … He'll go for it.'

Two seconds later, the English offie Richard Dawson dances in, flights his spinning orb towards Waugh … pitching just outside the off-stump … while the crowd hangs in suspended animation … as it lands and snarls up … as Waugh moves … on to his back foot … and CRACKS it … straightintothefence!

Shear pleasure

Federated Farmers of New Zealand spokeswoman Jeanette Maxwell says shearing's time has come: 'Surely, the time has come to elevate shearing's sporting status to the ultimate world stage? One way would be to make shearing a demonstration sport at a Commonwealth Games, if not the Olympics itself … Top shearers are athletes who take it to another level.'

Cue the boys up the back: 'Shearing? Shearing? I'm not shearing my sheep with anyone!'

A short trip to the centre

In the 1972 Ashes tour of England, the great Dougie Walters had a horror stretch. How bad was it? Pretty bad.

Just after he went out to bat in the Test at Lord's the dressing-room phone had rung. It was his mother, calling all the way from Dungog.

Dennis Lillee picked up the phone. 'I'm sorry, Mrs Walters, but Doug has just this moment gone in to bat.'

'That's all right, Dennis,' Mrs Walters replies. 'I'll hold …'

Ken's slice of life

Channel Nine's sports guy Ken Sutcliffe's most memorable moment?

It was when a story was presented concerning golfer Mianne Bagger and how she had started life as a man but, after an operation, was now a woman.

The final shot of the story showed Bagger hitting the ball awry. On handing back to the main newsreader, Mark Ferguson, Ken added with a smile: 'That's a very nasty slice ...'

Abba dabba

Sri Lankan seamer Dilhara Fernando had just been called for a no ball and had proceeded to question the umpire about his decision.

A fellow commentator asked Kerry O'Keefe what the umpire would be saying to Fernando in this situation.

In a beautifully deadpan manner, O'Keefe replied: 'I reckon he'd be saying, "If I had to do the same again, I would my friend, Fernando."'

Artie in short bursts

In the early '80s, playing league for the mighty Stanley Rivers Rugby League Club, a reader and his mates found themselves in a social match against the Moreton Bay Pub side, which was owned at the time by the great Arthur Beetson.

Although well and truly retired from professional football by this time, and terribly unfit, Artie played in this game and was his usual devastating self in the first half, always drawing in three or four frantic defenders, before effortlessly offloading and setting up his team mates.

At half time, however, the Stanley Rivers coach, Joey Chambers, brings his players in tight and, with a gleam in his eye, tells them quietly: 'When he gets the ball next time, just let him go through.'

Sure enough, early in the second half, near his own line, Artie gets the ball. Stanley Rivers players, just like Scipio's soldiers, step aside. Artie, like Hannibal's elephants, charges through. He runs three-quarters of the field before, pale and puffing like a sick rhinoceros in the desert, his legs start to wobble and, exhausted, he is cut down.

And that, friends, was the end of Artie for that game. He had to leave the field for want of breath!

Fit for a septic tank

Mean Machine member Neil Brooks was once at a championship meeting in the US and was up against a brash, in-your-face and trash-talking American who, before the race, was expending considerable energy trying to psych him out, including the usual stuff about his sexual orientation and parentage, etc.

Brooks refused to respond in any way but, when on the blocks, jumped the start—to the sniggers of that same American. However, instead of simply turning around and going back to his starting block, Brooks ducked under the rope into the American's lane and ever so slowly swam back to the edge of the pool.

He then lifted himself out of the water and walked past the American and whispered to him, 'I've just pissed in your lane', before going on to win the race against the still thunderstruck Yank.

RAH! And no, I have no idea whether it's true, but it definitely should be!

Sydney cheek travels the world

Reader Warwick Broad was recently visiting Pisa in Italy and was dining with his girlfriend at a restaurant when a woman of Asian ethnicity approached them.

'Are you Australians?' she asked, having overheard them and noted their accents.

When they confirmed that they were, the very friendly lady asked them a few questions about the best restaurants they'd been to in Pisa, etc, as she was looking for a nice place to go with friends. Then ...

'What state are you from?' she asked.

'NSW.'

'My son used to play cricket for NSW ...,' she said, heading off into the night.

'Good night, Mrs Chee Quee,' our reader said.

'How did you know her name?' his girlfriend asked, mystified.

Price of fame

Here is a classic exchange between Darrell Eastlake and Jack Gibson during a long-ago State of Origin match.

Eastlake, shouting: 'What about Ray Price, Jack? He wouldn't know the meaning of the word "fear"!'

Silent pause.

Gibson, absolutely deadpan, 'There's a few other words he doesn't know the meaning of.'

Princess fails test

Smokin' Joe French—a grizzled old Queenslander, burnt brown by the northern Australian sun, and forever sucking on a Marlboro—was one of the great men of Australian rugby. As President of the Australian Rugby Union during the late 1980s and early 1990s, he found himself sitting in the Royal Box, beside Princess Diana, during the World Cup Final held at Twickenham on 2 November 1991.

Of course royal protocol demanded that he not be allowed to smoke for the whole two hours that the game and subsequent official ceremony went on. It was for this reason that, when the (victorious) Wallabies finally made it back to their dressing room and everyone was in a delirium of victory, Smoking Joe rather stood out. For, instead of joining in, there he was in the corner, trying to ease the agony of his tortured lungs by sucking on *two* Marlboros at once!

'Well, Joe,' the assistant coach said to him, 'you've just spent two hours sitting beside the most beautiful woman in the world, and we all want to know: what is Princess Diana really like?'

Smoking Joe took another deep drag on his cigarettes, peered through the pungent grey clouds and immortally replied in his gravelly voice: 'She knows f**k-all about rugby.'

A different perspective

England's recent defeat by Iceland reminds me of a similar shock result in 2002, when Scotland drew 2-2 with the Faroe Islands (pop. 50,000).

A caller to Radio Scotland went on a five-minute rant about how badly the team had played against such feeble opposition, and suggested forcefully that players and coach should be summarily shot.

The commentator agreed, saying that it was certainly the most dismal performance he had ever seen from a Scottish team.

Caller (shocked): 'I'm not Scottish, I'm a Faroe Islander!'

Running with the balls

A man travels to Spain and goes to Pamplona during the great Running of the Bulls festival.

On his first day there, he goes out late for dinner at a restaurant in the centre of town. He orders the house special and is brought a plate with potatoes, corn and two large meaty objects.

'What's this?' he asks.

'*Cojones, señor,*' the waiter replies.

'What are *cojones*?' the man asks.

'*Cojones,*' the waiter explains, 'are the testicles of *el toro*—the bull who lost at the arena this afternoon.'

At first, the man is disgusted, but being the adventurous type he decides to try this local delicacy. To his amazement, it is quite delicious. In fact, it is so good that he decides to come back again the next night and order it again. This time, the waiter brings out the plate, but the meaty objects are much smaller.

'What's this?' he asks the waiter.

'*Cojones, señor,*' the waiter replies.

'No, no,' the man objects. 'I had *cojones* yesterday and they were much bigger than these.'

'*Señor,*' the waiter explains in his thickly accented, sleepy Spanish voice, 'the bull does not lose every time.'

Cue jumper

It is the opening of the Los Angeles Olympics in 1984, and just as President Ronald Reagan swaggers to the podium with that very, very vague look on his face, the Olympic athlete bearing the torch runs up the steps past him to light the Olympic cauldron behind: *fa-fa-fa-FOOM!*

The people roar, the Olympic flag waves in the breeze, and Reagan starts in on his speech: 'Errr ... uhhh ... nnngh.' He stops, suddenly crestfallen, as the electric buzz in the stadium falls away to nothing.

Just then a tinny voice can be heard, hissing, sotto voce, 'Mr President, Mr President, just read your cue-cards, Mr President.'

The Olympic flag waves in the breeze, and Reagan's face suddenly lights up, newly confident.

'Ohhh,' he begins again. 'Ohhhh ... ohhhh ... ohhhh ... ohhhhh.'

And then the tinny voice is back: 'Mr President, you dickhead, you're reading the Olympic flag ...'

A pearl of wit

A friend tells me that a few years back he was on an evening flight from Tokyo to Hawaii on Japan Airlines and just after take-off the following announcement came over the intercom, in a soft wispy voice.

'This is Captain Takenata, speaking. We hope you enjoy your flight. We have a journey of 3000 kilometres to make and will be cruising at an altitude of 10,000 metres. We will be arriving over Honolulu at dawn tomorrow morning. And they don't know we're coming …'

Let your hair down

Reader John Harvey, concerned that the A-League is still not garnering enough attention from us in the mainstream media, provided a helpful list of things the players could do to improve this deplorable situation. They included:

1. Following each game, teams should go on a drinking binge. The team that ultimately wins the competition must be prepared to continue this activity for a minimum of five days;

2. One player should be nominated as the team comedian. He would be required to carry out hilarious practical jokes, such as using his roommate's shoes as the toilet;

3. One group should go out of its way to pick a fight with some of the locals—this is to be a mandatory activity for 'away' teams; another group to be responsible for using a mobile phone to make obscene phone calls to young girls in the middle of the night;

4. Immediately upon retirement, players who have popped pills to enhance performance during their careers (preferably without having been caught) and/or fathered an illegitimate child (preferably as result of a one-night stand when drunk) will be required to write a book about their experiences.

I know, I know, this is not the stuff of the usual PR program, but it really has worked for some codes.

Darts mouth

Having had fun over the years with the quotes of the great BBC darts commentator Sid Waddell, I was saddened to hear of his death in August 2012. Here are some of his best-loved quotes:

'Darts players are probably a lot fitter than most footballers in overall body strength.'

'There's no one quicker than these two tungsten tossers.'

'The atmosphere is so tense, if Elvis walked in with a portion of chips … you could hear the vinegar sizzle on them.'

'Even hypotenuse would have trouble working out these angles.'

'Steve Beaton—the Adonis of darts, what poise, what elegance—a true Roman gladiator with plenty of hair wax.'

'It's like trying to pin down a kangaroo on a trampoline.'

'He may practise twelve hours a day, but he's not shy of the burger van!'

Some club

A big-game hunter is walking through the Central African jungle one day when he wanders into a clearing and is surprised to find a pygmy standing proudly beside a big, dead elephant.

Amazed, he says, 'Crikey! Did you kill that, mate?'

The pygmy answers proudly, 'Yes, sir, I did.'

'How could a little bloke like you kill a big elephant like that?' he asks.

The pygmy replies, 'It was easy. I killed it with my club.'

The astonished hunter says, 'Wow! How big is your club?'

The pygmy answers, 'There's about sixty of us.'

Chancing your arm

Thirty years ago, my French rugby team journeyed to Paris to take on Racing Club de Paris. We gave it absolutely everything we had, tore at them from first to last, but ended up losing 62 points to nil, on a day when we were frankly lucky to get to nil.

Morose, we piled back into the bus. As the lights of Paris fell behind, I started bending the ear of our captain and inside centre, Eric Blanc, telling him exactly where I thought our backline was going wrong, how they should run straighter, do shorter-passes and do some loop-the-loop running as I had long seen the Ella brothers do.

Eric put up with it for as long as he could and then snorted, *'Mais Fitzzzeee, qu'est-ce que tu sais? T'es un avant, tu vois le match avec ton cul!'* ('But Fitzy, what would you know? You are a forward, you see the match through your arse.')

Merv's serve

Brilliant but enraging Pakistani batsman Javed Miandad loved nothing more than to get under the skin of his opponents.

His niggle worked particularly well against Australia, who never missed an opportunity to take the bait and be provoked. Who could forget the iconic image of Miandad raising his bat at Dennis Lillee with umpire Tony Crafter in the middle?

Lillee had retired, but in his place was Merv Hughes, a fiery Victorian who was never going to be accused of taking a backwards step.

The two were at each other the whole day like Punch and Judy. Miandad called Merv 'a fat bus conductor', but then broke the cardinal sin of sledging, which is Never Get Out. This gave Merv the chance to have the final word.

As a distraught Miandad began his long walk back to the pavilion, Hughes was slightly in his way, demanding 'Tickets please!'

Old South Africa

Back in 1992, when the Wallabies arrived in South Africa for the first time in a generation, captain Nick Farr-Jones was sitting up the front of the bus as it made its way to the team hotel in Pretoria. Looking around at the new city, he asked the South African liaison officer the population of Pretoria. 'About 300,000,' came the reply.

'Only 300,000?' queried Farr-Jones. 'Gee, it looks a lot bigger than that.'

'Well,' the white South African replied, 'it's three million if you count the blacks.'

———

Roy Masters tells a story concerning George Pippos, a famously acerbic Queenslander on the ARU board, who was not famous for his diplomatic niceties. When Pippos met South African president FW de Klerk, he asked bluntly, 'How many white fellas?'

'Around four million,' came the reply.

'How many black fellas?' Pippos continued.

'Around 28 million,' the president returned.

Pippos couldn't help himself: 'Jeez, you're f***ed.'

Four-letter context

A few years ago, at Parramatta Local Court many a magistrate threw out a charge against a man for calling police 'f***ing cops'. The judge's gavel came down and he formally found that, in this day and age, this kind of language is not offensive.

This caused some angst from the gobsmacked police and the very senior police prosecutor whose case it was. But moving on.

The next defendant was duly called three times outside the court; however, he did not appear. Deadpan, the police prosecutor formally reported this fact to the magistrate, 'No f***ing appearance, Your Worship.'

Somewhat taken aback, the magistrate composed himself and replied, 'Point taken ...'

Winning formula

On the eve of the Rugby World Cup Final of 1995 in Johannes-burg, I jagged an interview with mate and former opponent, All Black captain, Sean Fitzpatrick. The All Blacks had been impe-rious throughout the tournament thus far, led by their stunning winger, Jonah Lomu.

At the end of the interview Sean showed me a fax he had just received from an eight-year-old lad from a farm just outside of Christchurch:

Dear All Blacks,
Remember, rugby is a TEAM game.
All 14 of you, pass the ball to Jonah!
Chris (8)

Beyond starlight

The Melbourne *Age*'s Geoff McClure reports that whenever Michael Jordan meets Australians he tells them of the time he met an Australian woman at the New York Plaza hotel in 1998.

The woman, Margaret Kelly of Camberwell, met his airness in a lift and they chatted amiably as it descended to the foyer.

Just before they got out, Margaret commented on how tall Jordan was, saying: 'You should play basketball.' True story.

———

One month after the victorious 1999 World Cup campaign, John Eales went to Byron Bay with his wife Lara and son Elijah for some precious R & R.

Eales was standing in a supermarket queue when two kids ran up and asked for his autograph. As he obliged, an old fellow just ahead of him in the queue turned around and looked up, way up, at John. It turned out he had a stutter

'Are you w-w-w-with the w-w-w-w-w-w . . .?'

John helpfully broke in: 'Am I with the Wallabies?'

The fellow looked perplexed. 'No, no, no, are you w-w-w-w-w-with the w-w-w-w-Wiggles?'

Any which way but lose, Wayne

Wayne Bennett, at a press-conference, put forward the revolutionary view that Australians had no right to expect their sporting teams to win all the time, and therefore Australian coaches should be given a break: 'It's ridiculous ... You've got to understand the business that we're in. We play sport and there are losers. Someone has to win and someone has to lose and Australia—regardless of whatever sport they're in—are not going to stay at the top of everything for the rest of our lives. So you better get used to it.'

No, we won't, Mr Bennett, and you can't make us! We are Australians, dammit, and on the Australian National Charter it not only sez we have a right to eat too much turkey on Christmas Day, the right to say, 'How they hangin', mate?' to any bastard we ever meet, be he president or pauper, and the right to bore people from other countries absolutely rigid about how great Vegemite is; it also sez we have a right to expect perpetual victories against other nations, most particularly England and New Zealand, and it is our unquestioned right to whinge about it loud and long afterwards when we do lose while implying that, if only we were coach, the team would have won!

Bending with Beckham

'Why is it that when David Beckham has an alleged affair it is "steamy", and when he travels to Madrid he "jets" there, whereas my mate in Auckland's affair was sordid and when he goes to see his lawyer in Wellington he flies?' *Herald* letter writer, Harry Craven.

———

Perhaps the most famous quote of David Beckham, who retired last week: 'We're definitely going to get Brooklyn christened, but we don't know into which religion.'

———

Barry Humphries on what he gave the 84-year-old Rupert Murdoch and his three-decades younger bride, Jerry Hall, as a wedding present:

'David Beckham, and some jumper leads …'

Signs of the times

It was perhaps the most embarrassing evening of my life. There we were at a black-tie fundraiser for the Leukaemia Foundation in 2007, just before the Wallabies left for the World Cup. At the end of the night MC Buddha Handy came up with an idea. Referring to a woman in the corner, who had been painting a rugby tableau all evening he said, 'Everyone here who has played international rugby, come forward, sign your name, and the era in which you played.'

First man up was the great Dr Marcus Loane and, as the cameras zoomed in, his beautifully florid signature was thrown up on the big screen:

Dr Mark Loane 1972-1982
How the crowd clapped.
And now,
Nick Farr-Jones (1984-1993)
And
David Campese (1982-1996)
Then, just before me, a Wallaby whose career had spanned
    THREE decades, and TWO millenia:
Tim Horan—(1989-2001)
Ah, how the crowd cheered.
And now, humbly, it is my turn.
What else could I do?

I signed:

Peter FitzSimons (July)

—

But what a July it was! And what a back-line the Wallabies boasted at the time!

Nick Farr-Jones at half-back, Michael Lynagh at five-eighth, Tim Horan at inside-centre, Jason Little at outside centre, David Campese at self-centre ...

Heroic twofer

Following Shane Warne in London being caught by *News of the World* cavorting with a couple of likely lasses, in the middle of an Australian series, there was the usual hell to pay, with your humble correspondent piling on with the best of them. But Warne was not without support. I quickly received the following letter.

Dear Fitz,
Well, well, well, what about poor old Warney then—I just think it's terribly unfair that the media would ignore the 7-99 he takes on a Sunday for Hampshire, but make a big deal of the two for 69 he bagged the night before.
Boom. Boom.
Kind regards,
Chris Ogge

Mixed-metaphor madness

Our first contestant, representing New Zealand, is Crusaders lock, Ross Filipo, who shared with the Kiwi media his thoughts on facing the No. 6 for the Hurricanes, Jerry Collins. Speak up, young Ross, if you would:

'Jerry and the boys might come hammer and tongs but we just have to fight fire with fire, I guess.'

We love it, Ross! Now let's go to the score. The American judge likes it, awarding him an eight out of ten; the Swiss judge marks down a seven for Ross; and the German judge gives him only a five on the grounds of being a pedant ... but remember, they always tend to mark low.

OK, up against him we have Mark Geyer, representing Australia. On Triple M's football call as Cronulla played the Roosters, Geyer boldly attempts, ladies and gentlemen, a double-cliche, double-metaphor, all in the one sentence. Degree of difficulty: 2.2!

Quiet now ... How do you think the Cronulla halfback is going, Mark?

'There is nothing better in rugby league than seeing Brett Kimmorley take the bull by the scruff of its horns ...'

Got him! American, Swiss and German judges all agree on an eight out of ten.

Every nose
has a silver
grindstone

Fun, games and Gough

As part of the bid process for the Sydney Olympics, AOC president Coates hired an aircraft and pilot and criss-crossed Africa, pressing the flesh of dignitaries of African sports associations, Olympic committees and IOC members in return for crucial votes. To add gravitas, Coates took Gough and Margaret Whitlam—a master stroke, as Gough was so much admired throughout Africa for his anti-apartheid stand.

One night they were in the back of the African beyond, dining under the stars, when a local journalist stood up from the table and relieved himself only a short distance from the table. Gough didn't blink.

'Didn't that bother you Gough?' Coates asked.

'No comrade,' the great man replied. 'Just another media leak.'

Aussie Rules—there are no rules

Let's hear it for Aussie Rules. After a decade or so of bagging it, and another decade of feeling lukewarm at best, I have finally come to the conclusion that its beauty lies in the fact that it really is the most quintessentially Australian game of all.

1. Despite the name, there don't really seem to be any rules to speak of. At least not very complex ones whereby the only person that truly understands them is the umpire. *As a people, we've never been too big on rules, and this game isn't either.*

2. Most other sports, and particularly union and league, have an obsession with whether a player, or the ball, did or did not go beyond the boundary line. Not Aussie Rules. Even in grand-finals no one seems to give a stuff as they scamper right along the line. *Close enough is good enough. Keep going!*

3. Every other football code has an offside rule. Not Aussie Rules. *You're an Australian, mate. Go where you damn well please!*

4. As far as the scoring system goes, every other football code says you either did score, or you didn't. Not Aussie rules. If you get the ball between the two big posts—beauty, take six points. But if you just miss, no worries. You had a go, and you had a bloody good go, so take a point anyway! *Aussie Rules—the only sport in the world where you get a point, just for having a go!*

I love this country

It was a great Australian moment. Not quite like mother used to make, but still very good.

It was the semi-final of the 2015 World Cup between Australia and India in Sydney. Straight after an Indian batsman had been given out, the camera pans to a 20-something Indian woman, dressed in the colours of her nation of birth, but whose outlook now clearly owes something to Australia.

'Ah, bullshit ...' says she.

Energy savers

This guy—let's call him Big Jack—goes for a swim on Christmas Day at Manly Beach, and is standing on a sandbank in chest-deep water when a sudden surge sweeps his feet out from under him, to take him seawards in a strong rip. Not panicking, but swimming hard, of course he looks to the shore, where he can see the lifesavers watching him intently and ... chatting earnestly. But not actually doing anything.

Still not panicking, he keeps swimming hard until, finally, exhausted, his feet touch the sand again ... only to be swept away once more!

Same thing: he looks to the shore, and there are the lifesavers, all with their eyes on him, talking animatedly, and one or two pointing in his direction. And ... stroke. And ...... stroke. And .... stroke. One more time, his feet touch the bottom, and this time he gets purchase and manages to stagger to the shore where he sinks to the sunny sand.

A shadow falls across him. He looks up. There are the lifesavers. They have a six-pack of beer with them.

'Mate,' one of them says, giving him the six-pack, 'we were taking bets on whether we would have to come out and rescue you. You deserve this.'

Let's punctuate

Dear Fitzy,

Thought you might like to know that the Swans' stalwart defender Lewis Roberts-Thomson (nickname 'Hyphen') did not play against the Essendon Bombers. This was all to the good, as the Bombers forward playmaker Nick Kommer did play, and the poor punctuation would have spoiled the game.

After all, you can't have a Hyphen following a Kommer!

Regards,

Roger M. Hurley

Root of the matter

Really old readers might remember the controversy back in 1983 when Channel 9 tried jazzing up its cricket commentary by including the highly accomplished thespian Kate Fitzpatrick as a guest commentator for a Test match in Adelaide. The acclaim for the move was something less than universal, prompting letters to the editor, talk-back calls, and endless complaints to Nine itself.

David Hill, the executive producer of the cricket coverage at the time and the man who hired Fitzpatrick, later recalled:

The one thing that was unusual as this disaster unfolded around me day by day was that there was not one phone call from Kerry [Packer]. But the night I get home from Adelaide after the Test, the phone rings.

Kerry: It's Packer here.

Hill: Mr Packer, how are you?

Kerry: I don't have any comment whatsoever on your latest exploit. I just have a question.

Hill: Yes?

Kerry: Is she a good f**k?

Hill: Mr Packer, I really wouldn't know.

Kerry: In that case, son, you've missed out both ways.

He scores a goal, starts running around flapping his arms, then he just, takes off...!!

Celebration ripe with meaning

One thing that has always given me the ragings about international soccer is all the nonsense that goes on when some booger scores. You know, all that contrived hysteria. The scorer's manic waving of the arms. His lack of acknowledgement of whoever it was who fed him the pass from which he scored. The running to the adoring fans. The pursuit by the teammates. The grapple tackle to the ground, while the rest of the team piles on top.

Always the same vainglorious self-obsessed hoo-ha. But wait!

Last Sunday, when Roma played Lazio in a Serie A derby, striker Francesco Totti slotted in a beauty for Roma, as his heavily pregnant wife watched on. In her honour, Totti recovered the ball, put it under his jersey and ran to her part of the grandstand, where he lay on the grass in front. When his teammates caught up, it was their job to 'deliver' the ball, before holding it triumphantly aloft as the Italian crowd did what an Italian crowd always does best—went completely nutso in ecstasy.

For my money, that is right up there with that terrific occasion when Mark Riddell was playing for St George Illawarra and, after scoring a scorcher of a try just in front of the dead-ball line, vaulted the fence a split second later, took his place in a front-row seat and applauded the four-pointer along with everyone else.

Humour! Spark! Originality!

The odd cuss is always par for the course

The annual awards night at the Jamberoo Golf Club boasts a major award for the most interesting or amusing incident by a member on a course during the year.

Lyn Deegan had been playing in a ladies' competition at Bowral Golf Club, when she couldn't help but notice that one of her playing partners was becoming so impatient with anything less than a perfect shot that she kept muttering loudly, 'F it!' ... 'F it!'

By the third hole this was becoming too much for Lyn, who suggested to her partner that, if it would make her feel better, she should let it all out, and scream just once 'F**k it!'

Came the icy reply: 'My dear, I was saying: Effort, effort!'

It's heaven or the trophy, not both

Back in 2002, late one Sunday evening just after the Warriors had killed off his team's chances for another year, they reckon an avid Sharks fan walked into a church at Cronulla and gets down on his knees.

'God,' he says, 'in 35 years, we've never won the comp. Three out of the last four years, we've got to one game short of the grand-final and fallen over. God, why do you hate us so much? Why have you so forsaken us?'

There is momentary silence as the last echoes of the supplicant's words bounce around the rafters. Then a frustrated voice booms out:

'Jeez, mate. I've given you the Sutherland Shire to live in, a little slice of heaven on earth! What more do you want!'

Mighty Merv and the Don

Back in the late-1980s, when the West Indies were at the height of their powers, it was a point of honour with them to pick eleven fast-bowlers in every side. Some of them could bat, too, but the starting point was fast-bowlers. The wicket-keeper was a fast-bowler, the manager, was a fast-bowler, the *bus-driver* was a fast-bowler.

Led by Malcolm Marshall, Curtly Ambrose, Courtney Walsh and Patrick Patterson, they mostly made short work of Australian batsmen, and on the 1988/89 tour, already had the series well in the bag as they headed for the final fifth Test in Adelaide.

How stunning it was, then, near the conclusion of Australia's first innings, when Merv Hughes came in to face the might of the West Indies attack and gave extraordinary resistance! Instead of poking, or prodding, or offering a straight bat, Merv started swinging. Sometimes he hit, sometimes he missed, twice he snicked it and was dropped, three times he snicked it over the slips cordon ... to finish the day at 72 not out! Now the tradition in Test cricket, of course, is for the batting side to take a few beers into the dressing room of the fielding side, to discuss the day's events.

Not on this day. Merv takes two full eskies! He is going to give them blow-by-blow a full account of his innings, tell them how it felt for him and ask them how it felt for them? This is all going swimmingly, at least for Merv, as the West Indians get in and out of the showers, when suddenly a hush falls across the room.

It is Sir Don Bradman himself, being ushered into the room by cricket officials from South Australia. Of course each West Indian player stands up before the great man comes near him, shake his hand, in the sure knowledge that one day, they will be able to tell their grandchildren, that one time, they met the great Sir Donald Bradman.

When, however, Bradman finally gets to the last man on the bench, it is to find the most fearsome fast bowler of the lot, Patrick Patterson—two metres tall of pure, whip-cord steel, who has just emerged from the shower and is resting his weary bones—still seated before him.

The whole room falls quiet at the awkwardness of it, wondering what will happen.

Finally, 30 seconds or so later, Patterson stands up, towers over the diminutive Sir Donald, squints down upon him and says: '*You* Sir Donald Bradman? YOU Don Bradman??? I kill you, maan! I bowl at you, I kill you! I split you in two!'

Bradman looks Patterson in the eye and coolly replies: 'You couldn't even get Merv Hughes out. You'd be no chance against me, mate!'

Funny game, cricket

That story has a corollary. For also in the dressing room that evening is Dean Jones, who has actually also knocked out a century on the day. Sir Donald is rarely locquacious, but on this day, he digs deep, smothering Jones with compliments.

Merv Hughes hovers close, like a kid on Christmas morning, waiting to unwrap his presents. Surely, Sir Donald must acknowledge his own efforts with a kind word, and whatever he says will be something to treasure forever!

Finally, Sir Donald turns to go, catches sight of Merv, pauses a moment, stares at him, and then mutters, shaking his head, 'Yeah, it's a funny game, cricket!'

A dog of a session

I am reliably told the Waratahs have all been issued with heart-rate monitors similar to a watch which, after exercise, can download data into a computer to measure resting heart rates, heart rates during exercise, rate of recovery, etc. In addition to the scheduled team training, each player must do a session by themselves each day with the monitor on when their heart rate goes over a certain level. One day last week, after one player handed in his monitor and the info was downloaded, the medical staff suddenly became seriously alarmed. They urgently called the player and asked if he had done his additional training.

'Yes ...' he replied, looking perhaps a little strained.

'What did you do?' they asked.

'A big sprint session down at my local park ...' On and on the questioning went, until the player asked what the problem was. The problem was the monitor was showing a report of 300 beats per minute at which rate, the human body long ago blew up. It turns out the player had strapped the monitor onto his rottweiler and made it chase balls for the session.

Photo finish

Back in 1982, see, when they were filming the climactic scene for the film *Phar Lap*, they hired a couple of dozen actual jockeys to gallop their charges across the line, in a ten-camera shoot, and ...

'And CUT!'

The director gathers the jockeys in, just after they have charged across the finish, exactly as requested.

'Gentlemen,' he says, 'that was perfect, in every detail, bar one thing. The camera taking the front-on shot malfunctioned, and we didn't get that key bit of footage. I am terribly sorry to ask you this, and don't even know if it is possible, but we really need you to do the whole thing again, but ... but you have to finish in exactly the same order, in exactly the same formation, with exactly the same distance between you as this time ...'

There is a moment's stunned silence, and then the lead jockey speaks for them all.

'What exactly,' he says, 'is the problem?'

AC/DC

I knew that sports journalism was going to be my kind of thing when shortly after joining the *Sydney Morning Herald* I heard the story of a former member of the sports section who was a notably big drinker and prone to being rather loud about it. When the first State of Origin game was played in Brisbane in 1980, our hero found himself for a week at the Brisbane Travelodge with an open expense account, open mini-bar fridge and open-door policy for every rugby-league identity and acquaintance he had in town. And nor did he worry about such niceties as sleep, which in his view was for weak men only.

Now it so happened that the rock band AC/DC was in town at the same time and staying at the same hotel, and … well … I am proud to report that after three days of being just down the corridor from our big-drinking sports journo and his equally hard-drinking mates … AC/DC complained!

Porn video

It was a wonderful thing, in late 1985, to find myself suddenly living in the French heartland, playing rugby for Brive for the next four years, while living in the nearby tiny village of Donzenac. The rugby was exhilarating, the people warm, the cuisine and wine superb. My teammates though? They were a bit … odd. Wonderful men, and fantastic players, but, still a bit odd.

I first realised how odd, about ten weeks in. Every second week, see, we would play away games, sometimes as far as five or six hours away on the bus, and the return trip would always see us getting back to Brive very late on the Saturday night. And one tradition never varied, I discovered. About an hour out from Brive, a porn video would be put on the bus VCR, to get the lads in the mood for hitting Brive's one disco, *La Charrette*, where we knew many of the town's more enthusiastic female rugby fans awaited. All well and good. Ish. Just a bit ODD. But one night, after beating the Perpignan side in a thriller, disaster struck. Jean-Francois had just put on the porn video at midnight, and the boys had crowded up the front, when suddenly smoke comes from the VCR and the screen goes blank! Exactly what had been happening on the screen had now happened to the whole video system, and it was clearly beyond repair. A dark pall settles over the whole bus. What to do?

And then like a shaft of light from the heavens, it happened. Up ahead in the gloom, as we passed through Sarlat and got onto the windy road just north of there, we see another bus up ahead in the distance. It is the lads of the nearby town of Tulle, our most bitter rivals! But forget that enmity now, for Jean-Francois is the one who sees it first.

Of course! They are watching a porn video too, and if you lean in close, you can just see through our front window, and their rear window, thrusting buttocks!

Jean-Francois has a word to Mikay, the bus driver, who grunts his agreement, and within 30 seconds has brought the front of our bus to within five metres of the back of their bus, even as Mikay flashes his light and bips his horn to get their attention.

In some kind of French sign language that completely escapes me, Jean-Francois tells the Tulle lads what has happened, and what we need and they instantly comply—all of them lowering themselves in their seats as far as they can go, so as to allow the Brive boys an unimpeded view of the action.

And so it goes through the night, the keenest ones of the Brive team with their noses pressed against the windscreens, the Tulle boys with their heads down, and the two buses proceeding happily through the night, along winding roads at 100 km/h just five metres apart. And no-one, bar one gobsmacked Australian up the back, blinks!

They are a weird mob, not us!

Buck

Waiting

In the mid-1980s, I played my one and only game at No. 8 for the Waratahs against the touring All Blacks. I was given one instruction: stop 'Buck' Shelford, the rampaging superstar who had just burst onto the international rugby scene. Yes, boss. Friends, I am not proud of what happened that day at Concord Oval in Sydney's Inner West. For 80 minutes, I hit Buck high, I hit him low. I hit him early, I hit him late. I hit him from in front, I hit him from behind when he wasn't looking. I even hit him when *I* wasn't looking! I scratched, I clawed. Still, *nothing* slowed that bastard down, and at game's end, the Waratahs had gone down by 30-odd points. These were still the days, mind, when there would be a reception at the end of each representative match, with speeches by both presidents and captains, and an exchange of ties, followed by a quick buffet, and so it was on this day. Shame-faced about what had happened on the field, and with my sanity now returned, I confess to feeling a little awkward, when Buck and I got to the last chicken drumstick on the platter at the same time.

I did the only thing I could do, which was to offer my hand and say,

'Buck, Peter FitzSimons, pleased to meet you.'

The great man took my hand, smiled, and was clearly quite sincere in his reply: 'Peter, pleased to meet you. Did you play today?'

Waiting, waiting

'Waiting for Cronulla to win a Premiership, is like leaving the porch light on for Harold Holt.'
Jack Gibson

Devil in the detail

Ka-Foom! The NRL coach looks up from his desk to find the Devil himself emerging from a puff of smoke.

'Here's the deal,' the Devil says without preamble. 'I am going to personally organise your team next season. Your five-eighth is going to play like Wally Lewis on a good day, your key forwards will between them boast the collective qualities of Artie Beetson, Ray Price and Cameron Smith. Every decision from the bunker will go your way, as will every bounce of the ball—but still the press will be sure to credit *you,* and you alone, with the genius of having formed up such an extraordinary side. In return, I want not only your soul but also those of your wife, your children, your children's children and all subsequent children for the next ten generations. Do we have a deal?'

The director, an experienced campaigner who is not easily fooled, is stunned, but also highly suspicious.

Leaning forward, he asks Lucifer: 'And what's the *catch*?'

Mistaken identity

From a northern NSW newspaper comes this story of a Tweed Heads couple who drove their car to Woolworths, only to have it break down in the car park. The man, the well-known prop for his local rugby club, tells his wife to carry on with the shopping while he fixes the car. The wife returns 20 minutes later to see a small group of people gathered around the bonnet of the car, staring down, goggle-eyed. On closer inspection, she sees a pair of male legs protruding from under the vehicle. The problem is that because he is dressed in baggy blue shorts on this stinking hot day, the man's obvious lack of underwear has turned his private parts into glaringly public ones. Red rigid with embarrassment, the wife nevertheless steels herself long enough to dutifully step forward, kneel and quickly put her hand UP his shorts, to tuck everything back into place. On regaining her feet, she looks across the bonnet and finds herself looking at her shocked husband who is standing idly by.

The man from the NRMA, meanwhile? He has to have three stitches in his forehead . . .

He is resting comfortably.

Ask a silly question

The opening fast bowler for the Petersham Cricket Club is commuting from Stanmore to his job in North Sydney. He's finished reading the morning paper and is saving it to give to friends on the job. So how do you save a newspaper on State Rail? You sit on it! A new commuter comes in, sees the newspaper under his rear end and asked the second most stupid question the fast bowler has ever heard:

'Are you reading that paper?'

The fast-bowler stands up, turns the page, sit right back down on the paper and answers ... 'Yes.'

They breed 'em smart in Sydney's Inner West.

The Lower North Shore? Not so much.

Tooth Fairy

The smart rugby union prop, the ethical rugby league manager, the impoverished Sheffield Shield cricketer and the Tooth Fairy are sitting around a table, beneath a single, swaying light bulb.

On the table before them is a $100 note. Suddenly the light goes off. When it comes back on ten seconds later, the money is gone.

Who took it?

The impoverished Sheffield Shield player, of course. The others are just figments of your imagination!

Through thick and thin

An old Test cricketer has been slipping in and out of a coma for several months, yet his wife has stayed by his bedside every single day. One day, when he comes to, he motions for her to come nearer. As she sits by him, he whispers, eyes full of tears:

'You know what, Becky? You have been with me all through the bad times. When I got that first terrible wrist injury keeping me out of top-level cricket for two years, just when my professional career began, you were there to support me. When I struggled through those long agonising months of rehabilitation, you were there. When I slipped in the shower, just when I was about to make my comeback, and broke my knee, you were by my side. When I finally made it back, all the way to the Test side, only to get two golden ducks and never play Test cricket again, you were there. And then, all through those last decades of struggling to make a living, given that I had sacrificed all for cricket, you were there. And now, as my health has slowly failed through these last ten years of agonising pain, you were still by my side ... Beck ... you know what?'

'What dear?' she gently asks, smiling as her heart begins to fill with warmth.

'You're a f***ing JINX.'

High and dry

GOTTA love this city. Tuesday's big news event was the crash of an America's Cup yacht into an Opera House that someone had so very carelessly left parked right on the very spot. But amid all the subsequent carnage, alarm, rescue and all the rest, one of the passengers as subsequent news photos showed, not only kept himself high and dry, but also seemed to have a beer securely in his hand. Gotta love this city!

Light weight

A singularly kind reader stopped TFF in the street the other day and claimed to have noted that your humble correspondent had taken off some weight in recent times. Thought you'd never notice! And I can tell you why, too. During the Olympics, TFF was doing some light palling around with one of my erstwhile biographical subjects, up at the wonderful Parthenon, when an awe-struck 20-something Australian tourist approached on the double. 'John Eales! John Eales!' he near shouted. 'You've been my hero since I was just a kid! Is there any chance I could have my photo taken with you?'

Eales graciously acquiesced, and the bloke, with a nod of vague recognition, handed the camera to me, asking would I mind? Not at all. Delighted. I took the shot. The bloke warmly pumped the former Wallaby captain's hand, saying, 'Thanks, John!' before turning to me.

'And thank you, too, Buddha!'

———

'They haven't even finished the Acropolis yet!'

Vince Sorrenti, giving dire warnings just before the Athens Olympics that it was never going to work.